iPhone 5

LYNN BEIGHLEY

D0910604

Peachpit Press

Visual QuickStart Guide
iPhone 5
Lynn Beighley

Peachpit Press
www.peachpit.com

To report errors, please send a note to: errata@peachpit.com
Peachpit Press is a division of Pearson Education.

Acquisitions Editor: Cliff Colby
Project Editor: Rebecca Gulick
Copy Editor: Liz Welch
Production Coordinator: David Van Ness
Compositor: Francisco Design
Proofreader: Patricia J. Pane
Indexer: Valerie Haynes Perry
Cover Design: RHDG / Riezebos Holzbaur Design Group, Peachpit Press
Interior Design: Peachpit Press
Logo Design: MINE™ www.minesf.com

ISBN-13: 978-0-321-90257-3
ISBN-10:   0-321-90257-2

9 8 7 6 5 4 3 2 1

Printed and bound in the United States of America

Dedicated to new iPhone users, about to discover what a powerful, useful, and fun device you now own.

Acknowledgements

You wouldn't be turning the pages of this book, or swiping through it on your iPad, if it weren't for the hard work and great skill of the following people:

Peachpit Press and Publisher Nancy Ruenzel, who trust me to write their books; Nikki McDonald, who pulled me, willingly, back into book writing; Cliff Colby, who had the right project for me at the right time; Rebecca Gulick, who herded my catlike self into getting it done; production coordinator David Van Ness, who pulled it from the mess I left it into this fine book with astonishing aplomb; patient copy editor Liz Welch, who cleaned up thousands of typos, scads of structural snafus, and much grammatical gibberish; Francisco Design, which made words and pictures into lovely pages; Patricia J. Pane, who proofread and saved me much embarrassment; and Valerie Haynes Perry, who skillfully created this book's invaluable index.

Table of Contents

Introduction

You may have just purchased your first iPhone, or perhaps you've been using iPhones for a while and upgraded to the iPhone 5 with iOS 6. Either way, there is likely lots you don't know about your new iPhone and its operating system. I've been an iPhone user for years. I thought I knew everything there is to know about it, but I learned many new things and discovered a ton of hidden features while writing this book.

The approach I've taken is to give you a thorough grounding in the tasks you most need and want to do with your iPhone—things like making calls, using email, and keeping track of appointments. But I've also covered how to use your iPhone to browse the web, watch movies, listen to music, play games, and numerous other things you may not have known your iPhone can do.

Basically, I present to you plenty of the meat and potatoes, but I've also tried to throw in an appetizer, a dessert, and a nice beverage. I've enjoyed writing this and learning more about the iPhone. I hope you'll have a few "Oh, wow!" moments of your own while you're reading this book.

About This Book

My intention in writing this book is to make it immensely useful for the person who is absolutely new to the iPhone. But I also include lots of great information for those of you who have used iPhones before.

The first five chapters take you through opening the iPhone box, knowing what the external controls do, performing some basic setup tasks, and making phone calls (along with all the nifty tricks you can perform with the phone part of your iPhone).

Chapters 6, 7, and 8 get you into the heart of the iPhone, and you'll learn about some of the special things your iPhone does well, such as Notifications, Siri, and apps.

The next few chapters get you doing things, like reading books and news, watching movies, playing games, taking photos, creating videos, writing emails, and sending messages.

Finally, the last two chapters give you a look at the odds and ends. These include other Apple apps, small but useful, and some really great Apple apps that you have to get from the App Store. Also, you'll learn about AirPrint and AirPlay, which let you print from your iPhone and stream media to your TV, respectively.

What You'll Need

It's pretty basic. You need an iPhone 5 with iOS 6. And it'll be helpful if you have a PC or Mac with the latest version of the free iTunes software. Finally, a Wi-Fi connection is needed if you want to make FaceTime calls. That's it.

Opening the Box

It's an exciting moment when you first open the box containing your new iPhone. You've been waiting to hold your new iPhone in your hands for a long time, and the moment has come. In just a moment you'll be holding your phone, probably one of the few times you'll see it completely bare, without that fancy case you bought for it.

Before you start adding apps, FaceTiming your friends, or chatting up Siri, let's take a look at your naked iPhone and the other goodies that came with it in that great little box.

In This Chapter

What's in the Box?

Open the box and gaze upon your shiny new iPhone. But don't get distracted. Before you play with it, take it out of the box and look at everything else you've gotten:

- A storage case containing a set of noise-canceling *Apple EarPods* with built-in remote control and microphone.

- *Lightning to USB cable*, used to recharge your iPhone or connect it to your computer to sync your iPhone with iTunes.

- *USB power adapter* that attaches to the USB end of your Lightning cable so you can recharge your iPhone from an outlet.

- Documentation.

- And of course, your *iPhone*.

Looking at Your iPhone

Take a look at your iPhone's hardware and specifications. **A** and **B** show you the front, side, bottom, and back of the iPhone. **Table 1.1** lists the iPhone specifications.

TABLE 1.1 iPhone Specifications

Specification	iPhone 5
Dimensions	4.87" x 2.31" x 0.30" (123.8mm x 58.6mm x 7.6mm)
Weight	3.95 ounces (112 grams)
Display size	4-inch (diagonal) Retina display
Display resolution	1136 x 640 pixels (326 pixels per inch)
Processor	A6 chip
Storage	16, 32, or 64 GB
Carriers	AT&T, Sprint, Verizon
Cellular and Wireless	GSM model: GSM/EDGE UMTS/HSPA+ DC-HSDPA CDMA model: CDMA EV-DO Rev. A and Rev. B LTE3 Wi-Fi (802.11a/b/g/n; 802.11n on 2.4 GHz and 5 GHz) Bluetooth 4.0 GPS and GLONASS
Battery life	Talk time: Up to 8 hours on 3G Browsing time: Up to 8 hours on LTE Up to 8 hours on 3G Up to 10 hours on Wi-Fi Standby time: Up to 225 hours
FaceTime Camera	1.2 megapixel photos 720p HD video
Backside illumination sensor	
iSight Camera	8 megapixel Autofocus Tap to focus LED flash Backside illumination sensor Five-element lens Face detection Hybrid IR filter f/2.4 aperture Panorama

A Controls on the front of your iPhone.

FaceTime camera

Sleep/Wake button

Receiver/front microphone

Ring/Silent switch

Status bar

Volume buttons

App icons

Multi-Touch display

iSight camera

Rear microphone

LED flash

Home button

B Back, bottom, and side of your iPhone.

Lightning connector

Headset jack

SIM card tray

Bottom microphone

Speaker

Turning It On and Off

When you're not using your iPhone, after a few minutes it will automatically go into a standby mode, or *sleep*. In sleep mode, the screen is off but your phone can still receive calls, texts, and even emails. Sleep mode also locks the screen so that an inadvertent tap won't end up with you accidentally calling your boss.

Sleep is usually sufficient, so you probably won't want to turn off your iPhone very often. If you don't want it ringing in a meeting or at the theater, you can put it to sleep and leave it in vibrate mode. But sometimes you might want to conserve the battery or reboot it.

Make your iPhone sleep

Your iPhone will go to sleep on its own after 1 minute. But to put it to sleep immediately, briefly press the Sleep/Wake button.

Wake your iPhone

Press either the *Sleep/Wake* or *Home* button and then slide the *slide to unlock* control on the screen **A**.

Power on your iPhone

Press and hold the *Sleep/Wake* button for a few seconds, until the silver Apple logo appears on the screen. You then will be on the lock screen. Slide the *slide to unlock* control (**A**).

Power off your iPhone

Press and hold the Sleep/Wake button for a few seconds, until a red "slide to power off" control appears on the screen. Drag the slider to off.

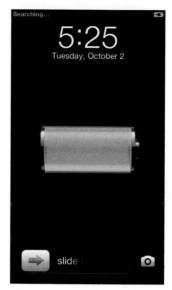

A The *slide to unlock control* appears when you power up your iPhone or press the Home button to reach the lock screen.

TIP If you want to protect your iPhone from other people, you can configure a password that you have to enter when you turn the power on or unlock the screen. You'll learn how to add a password to your iPhone in Chapter 3, "Setting Up Your iPhone."

A Low battery alert.

Charging Your iPhone

Your iPhone probably had a pretty full charge when you got it, but it's a good idea to know how to recharge it before you start using it.

You can tell your battery is low in several ways. When your battery only has 20 percent of its charge remaining, you will get an alert **A**. Both when locked and unlocked, the status bar displays a low power indicator **B**. And a battery icon with a red bar to indicate low power displays on the lock screen **C**.

continues on next page

B Low battery indicator on status bar.

C Low battery and recharging indicator on lock screen.

When the iPhone is completely discharged, it won't come on at all when you press the Home button or try to power it up with the Sleep/Wake button.

To charge your iPhone, plug the small end of the Lightning adapter into the bottom of the iPhone. It can be charged from an outlet with the power adaptor or from a computer's USB plug.

When it's charging, the battery indicators on the lock screen and in the far right of the status bar display powering icons (C and D).

D Recharging indicator in the status bar on the Home screen.

Using the Home Button

There's only one button on the front of the iPhone **Ⓐ**, but it's an important one. It's called the Home button, and the name is appropriate. Usually when you press it, you end up on the main screen of your iPhone, known as the Home screen.

When you want to close an app, pressing the concave Home button takes you back to the Home screen. The apps on the iPhone remember where you left off when you press the Home button. For example, say you were typing a note in the Notes app and pressed the Home button. The next time you open it, you'll see the note you were writing.

continues on next page

Home screen ——

Home button ——

Ⓐ The Home button and Home screen.

Here are the main functions of the Home button:

- When you're in an app, press it to return to the Home screen.

- When you're already on the Home screen and press it, you reach the Spotlight screen. This is a search tool for finding things on your iPhone (more about this in Chapter 2, "Touching Your iPhone").

- When your iPhone is asleep (on standby), press the Home button to wake it up.

- Holding down this button activates Siri (see Chapter 7, "Talking to Your iPhone," for more about Siri).

- Press the button twice when your iPhone is asleep and you'll get to the Lock screen with controls for your camera and music playing **B**.

TIP How many times have you seen something you wanted to take a picture of quickly, but had to fumble with your phone to pull up your camera? This is a quick way you can snap a photo without unlocking your phone.

- Press the button twice on your Home screen, and you'll see the screen slide up to reveal a bar showing the apps you've used most recently. This is really handy (**C**).

B Press the Home button twice in the Lock screen to get these controls.

C Press the Home button twice on the Home screen to see your recently used apps.

Controlling Volume

There are three volume controls on the side of your iPhone. These are the Volume Up (+) and Volume Down (-) buttons, and a Ring/Silent sliding switch that you can use to mute your iPhone.

Increase the volume

Press the Volume Up (+) button repeatedly, or hold it down to raise the volume quickly.

Decrease the volume

Press the Volume Down (–) button or hold it to lower the volume more quickly.

Mute rings and alerts

Flip the Ring/Silent switch toward the back of the phone so that the orange indicator is showing, and your iPhone ringtones and alerts are muted. Flip the switch toward the front of the phone to turn it off and your iPhone is no longer muted.

TIP Music, movies, and other media are not muted.

Using the EarPods

Your iPhone came with a pair of very useful Apple EarPods. These consist of a stereo headset with a tiny microphone and volume control built into the cord coming from the right earphone.

To use the EarPods:

- To talk to Siri, press and hold the middle button until you hear a tone. (Read more about using Siri in Chapter 7.)

    Press the top of the remote control to turn up the volume, and press the bottom to lower it. If the screen is locked, a volume indicator appears on the lock screen (**A**). Each press will raise or lower the volume by one setting.

- Pause the current song or video by briefly pressing the middle control. Press it again to resume.

- Press the middle button twice quickly to jump to the next music track (or chapter if you're watching a movie), or three times to go back to the previous track (or chapter).

- Press the middle button three times and hold it on the third press to rewind.

- When you get a phone call, answer the phone by pressing the middle button, and hang up by pressing it again.

- You can decline a call by pressing and holding the middle button until you hear a beep.

- Use call waiting by pressing the middle button once when you're in the middle of a call to answer the second call.

A Volume indicator on the lock screen.

2

Touching Your iPhone

You've seen what's in the box, and no doubt you're itching to get started. In this chapter, you'll learn some of the most fundamental skills you need to know. First, you'll take care of a bit of necessary housekeeping by working through the startup screens. Then you'll learn all about touching your iPhone, including how to use the many gestures your touchscreen supports; how to type, cut, copy, and edit text; how to search your iPhone; and how to get the definition of a word.

In This Chapter

Walking Through the Startup Screens

The first time you use your iPhone, you have to go through some startup screens that gather information about you, activate your phone with your cellular carrier, and ask you about your preferences. It's possible that the place you purchased your iPhone will walk through the steps with you, but if not, here's how to do it.

TIP It's a good idea to make sure your iPhone is charged up before you go through the startup process. If you're not sure how, check out Chapter 1, "Opening the Box."

Conventions in this book

When this book tells you to do something on the screen, you'll see instructions like:

- Tap Settings > Notifications > Do Not Disturb > Scheduled > On

This means that you should open your Settings by tapping on it. Then tap the Notifications control. Then tap the Do Not Disturb control. Finally, slide the Scheduled control to On.

You'll see labels matching each step in the instruction.

Turn on your iPhone. Slide the Configure arrow at the bottom of the screen to the right. You'll be presented with a series of screens where you'll make choices.

If you make a mistake, you can tap the Back button on the upper left. Keep in mind that nearly all the choices you're about to make can be changed later.

After each choice, tap the blue arrow button in the upper right of your screen.

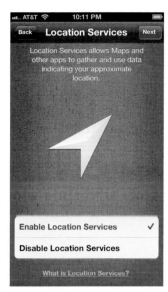

A Enable Location Services to allow your iPhone to know where you are and share that information with apps and services.

B Enter your Apple ID or create a new one. Your Apple ID is a user ID that will be used by Apple to let you make purchases in the App Store. It's also connected to your iCloud and iTunes accounts, among other things.

To set up your iPhone:

1. Choose a language by tapping on it.

2. Choose a country or region.

3. You can choose a Wi-Fi network if you like, but you don't have to. If you have an iPhone, you can wait for it to be activated.

4. Decide if you want to enable Location Services **A**. Location Services lets your iPhone share your location with apps and services. This is optional, but if you want to use Maps or the Find My iPhone feature, you'll need this turned on. (If you want to turn it on or off later, tap Settings > Privacy > Location Services and choose On or Off.)

5. Set up the device as a new iPhone, restore it from an iCloud backup, or restore it from an iTunes backup.

6. Sign in with an Apple ID, or create a new one if you don't currently have one **B**.

7. You'll see Apple's terms and conditions. You have to tap the Agree button to continue. This opens an alert confirming your choice. Tap Agree.

8. Decide if you want to use an iCloud account. iCloud is actually a collection of Apple services. An iCloud account lets you sync your data with other devices and computers. iCloud services are free.

continues on next page

9. If you don't use an iCloud account, you'll need to periodically back up your data with iTunes .

10. If you're worried about losing your iPhone, choose Use Find My iPhone to help locate it. This feature uses iCloud to let you track your device's location with a web browser or other iOS device.

11. If you signed in with an existing iCloud account, you'll see any email addresses associated with that account appear on the Messaging screen. Tap to deselect any addresses you don't want to work with iMessage and FaceTime.

12. Tap Use Siri . (If you want to turn it on or off later, tap Settings > General > Siri and choose On or Off.)

13. Choose whether or not you want to help Apple out by sending your Diagnostics & Usage information to them.

14. Finally, tap the Start Using iPhone screen to finish up.

C iCloud is a collective name for several free Apple services that use your cellular or Wi-Fi network to back up and sync your data with other devices and computers.

D Turn on Siri, your voice-activated personal assistant. (See Chapter 7, "Talking to Your iPhone," for more on using Siri.)

Using Multi-Touch Gestures

With only a few buttons, most of your tasks on the iPhone will be accomplished through your fingers on the screen. Here are the gestures that the iPhone understands and what they do.

- **Tap.** Gently tap the screen. Tapping is often used to launch apps, push buttons, flip objects around, or change to the next screen.

- **Tap and hold.** To edit text (see the section "Creating and Editing Text," later in this chapter), you'll use the tap-and-hold gesture. It will open a virtual magnifying glass or allow you to start cutting, copying, or pasting text.

- **Double tap.** This is often used to zoom in or out on an image or web page, or to return to a previous view.

- **Swipe/flick.** The swipe, or flick, gesture is when you rapidly and briefly brush your finger on the screen. This motion causes things to scroll up or down, or flip right and left through things (for example, album covers in Cover Flow view or sets of photos in the Camera app). The screen is responsive to the speed you are flicking. When you flick quickly, the iPhone keeps up by scrolling more quickly. If you want to stop the motion, just put your finger on the screen.

- **Drag.** If you want to move things like the flick does, but do it more slowly, try dragging your finger across the screen. This will control the speed of scrolling.

- **Stretch/pinch.** Stretching consists of using your thumb and index finger on the screen at the same time and moving them apart. Pinching is moving them back together. When looking at an image or web page, stretch to zoom in to it, pinch to zoom out.

- **Rotate.** Use your thumb and index finger as though you were going to pinch, but turn them clockwise or counterclockwise.

Opening and Closing Apps

Your iPhone lets you interact with one app at a time. Some apps can run in the background (see the next section "Multitasking"), but in general, you'll be working with a single app.

Most apps are effectively frozen when you switch away from them, but certain apps (such as Music and Mail) continue working in the background. Switching back to an app lets you resume where you left off.

To open an app:

- Tap the icon of the app you want to open.

To close an app:

- Click the Home button.

To force an app to close:

1. Press and hold the Sleep/Wake button. When the power-off screen appears, release the button.

2. Press and hold the Home button for several seconds. The Home screen appears. Unlock it. Your app should be closed.

   or

   Repeat Step 1, but this time drag the red slider to shut off your iPhone completely. Then restart it by holding down the Sleep/Wake button.

A This Dock displays the apps you've used most recently.

Multitasking

Though you can only work with a single app at a time, you can run certain apps in the background, such as Mail, Messages, or Music. And of course, no matter what you're doing, the Phone app is always running and can always receive calls.

The iPhone's ability to multitask allows you to change from one app to another and back again and keeps your work in both apps intact.

To multitask:

1. Double-click the Home button (this works both when you're using an app and when you're on the Home screen).

   The app you're in, or the Home screen, slides up. A Dock appears at the bottom of the screen. The Dock displays the apps you used most recently **A**.

2. To switch to another app, tap its icon in the dock.

3. When you want to go back to the first app, or switch to another one, double-click the Home button to open the Dock again.

> **TIP** The apps in the multitasking Dock appear in the order you last used them. You can use a left swipe or flick motion on the Dock to see even more.

continues on next page

The Dock contains more than just the apps you've recently used. If you swipe it to the right, it displays controls for your Music app **B** (read more about this app in Chapter 9, "Reading, Watching, And Listening "). There's also a control for locking the screen rotation (explained in Chapter 3, "Setting Up Your iPhone"). Swipe once more and you'll see the volume control **C**.

TIP Every app you've used at least once appears in the multitasking Dock. You may want to clean up the Dock periodically. You can remove icons from the Dock (not the apps themselves) by tapping and holding the icon in the Dock you want to remove until it starts to shake. Click the red Delete button. Be very careful not to do this on the Home screen, or you'll delete the actual app from your iPhone!

B Music controls and a Screen Rotation control are stashed in the multitasking Dock. Swipe to the right to see them.

C Swipe the multitasking Dock once more to the right to get to a volume control.

Shift key

Tap the **123** key to display numeric keyboard.

Tap the **#+=** key to display symbol keyboard.

Tap the **ABC** key to display standard keyboard.

Ⓐ These are the three keyboards you cycle through by tapping the button shown.

Creating and Editing Text

Whenever you open an app that expects you to type, an onscreen keyboard slides up. This onscreen keyboard has a number of important features you need to know about:

- There are three different keyboards built into one: the main keyboard, the numeric and symbol keyboard, and a third keyboard with even more symbols. Cycle through them by tapping keys on the left side of the keyboard **Ⓐ**.

- To type uppercase letters, tap the Shift key **Ⓐ**.

TIP Turn on Caps Lock by double-tapping the Shift key. The Shift key turns blue, and every letter you type will be capitalized. Turn it off again by tapping once on the Shift key.

- If you don't want to type, hide the keyboard by tapping outside of the text entry area.

- The Space, Return, and Delete keys behave as they do on any keyboard. You can hold down the Delete key to erase entire words at a time.

continues on next page

- To type a character with a special format (such as an umlaut or accent), tap and hold until a menu of choices appears **B**, then slide your finger to the character you want and release.

- If you turn your iPhone and your screen orientation is not locked, your keyboard will become wider to fit the screen **C** (see Chapter 3 for more about screen orientation).

- Your keyboard may change depending on which app you're using. For example, when you use Safari (see Chapter 9, "Reading, Watching, And Listening") and type in a URL, you'll see characters in the keyboard commonly used in web addresses **D**. You'll even see a .com key, which you can hold to see a menu of other domains, like .org or .net.

B This menu is revealed when you tap and hold on a character with special formatting.

C The keyboard widens to accommodate the screen when you turn the iPhone sideways.

D Your keyboard changes depending on which app you're using. When typing in a web address or URL, you can't use spaces, so the spacebar is gone, but a domain key, period, and slash are added.

A Tap the microphone key to begin dictating.

B While you're dictating, this control appears. Tap Done when you're finished.

Dictating Text

Most applications that accept text through the online keyboard also allow you to dictate to them. This includes Notes, Messages, Reminders, and Mail.

To use Dictation:

1. Make sure Siri is turned on in your Settings (Settings > General > Siri > On).

2. Open any application that lets you input text—for example, Notes.

3. Add a new note by tapping the + button in the upper right (learn more about using Notes in Chapter 12, "Creating").

4. Tap on the screen. The keyboard appears.

5. Tap the microphone key near the bottom left of the screen **A**.

6. A microphone control appears **B**. Start speaking and tap Done when you're finished. Your iPhone sends your recording to Apple headquarters to parse, and your words appear in the app a second or two later.

Dictating Punctuation

Though Dictation does a pretty good job of picking up your words, it doesn't know when you want to end a sentence, add a comma, or ask a question. But you can tell it. Speaking the name of the punctuation mark works. For example, to add a period, say "period." Saying "full stop" also works. Some of the most common signs and symbols that Dictation recognizes are the period, comma, question mark, exclamation point, semicolon, colon, quote, at sign, pound sign, ampersand, parentheses, plus sign, and minus sign.

Table 2.1 shows you a few more punctuation marks that your iPhone can understand.

TIP A few other useful expressions that Dictation understands are "new line," "new paragraph," and "all caps." Experiment to see what else you can discover!

TABLE 2.1 More Dictation Punctuation Marks

Say This	Get This
Left parenthesis	(
Right parenthesis	)
Ampersand	&
Pound sign	#
Question mark	?
Minus sign	–
Plus sign	+
At sign	@

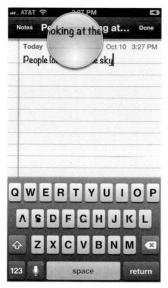

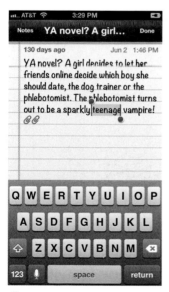

Selecting, Copying, and Editing Text

You're going to want to copy text from your apps from time to time, perhaps a line from an email or a snippet from a web page on the Safari app. Before you can copy text to paste it somewhere else, you need to select it.

To select text:

1. Open Safari and navigate to a web page.

2. Find the text you want to copy. Double-tap to zoom in the page.

3. Tap and hold next to the desired text. This opens the magnifier tool Ⓐ. Release and a word is selected Ⓑ.

continues on next page

4. Drag the blue selection dots on either side of the selected text to change what is selected 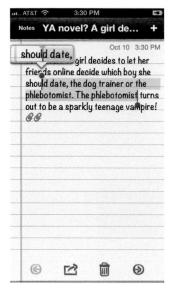. Drag the selection dots upward and downward if you want to select text above and below.

5. When you're done, tap Copy. Your text is saved in the iPhone clipboard and ready to be pasted somewhere.

TIP You can also cut text if you select text from something editable like the Notes app.

TIP If you want to edit text, you can select what you wish to edit and then begin typing over it.

Here are a few more useful tips to help you with selecting, editing, and copying text:

- When you're selecting text that you can also edit, tapping in the text field moves your cursor or insertion point to this location.

- You can move the insertion point by touching and holding. The magnifying glass appears. Drag your finger to the spot you want to insert text and then release.

- You can select an entire word by double-tapping it and choosing Select. Highlight an entire paragraph for selection by quickly tapping it four times.

C The blue circles on the right and left of the selected text can be dragged to change the selection area.

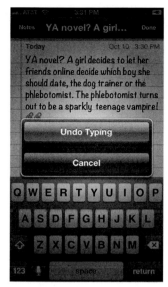

If you paste by mistake, shake your iPhone to open this Undo Paste window and tap Undo Paste.

Pasting Text

Once you've selected and copied text, you can paste it into other apps that allow text input.

To paste text:

1. Open any application, such as Notes, that lets you input text.

2. Double-click at the point where you want to paste the text.

3. Tap the Paste button

4. If you pasted by mistake, give your iPhone a firm shake. The Undo Typing window opens . Tap Undo Paste.

TIP You can copy and paste more than just text. You can also copy photos, images, videos, shapes, tables, and charts. For example, if you double-click and select an image, you can copy and paste that into any app that allows you to add images, such as an email you're composing in Mail.

Managing Keyboard Settings

Your iPhone has a whole page of settings for your online keyboard you can control. Open them by choosing Settings > General > Keyboard .

Here's what these settings do:

- **Auto-Capitalization.** Words that should be capitalized will be. These include proper nouns and words at the beginning of sentences.

- **Auto-Correction.** Your iPhone will watch for your typing errors and correct them for you.

- **Check Spelling.** You'll see a dotted red line under words you've misspelled. Tap on the word to see recommended spellings, and tap one to choose it.

- **Enable Caps Lock.** This setting allows you to double-tap the Shift key and turn on Caps Lock.

- **"." Shortcut.** When this is on, you can double-tap the spacebar at the end of a sentence and your iPhone will insert a period and a space.

Ⓐ These are the settings for your online keyboard. To get to these, tap Settings > General > Keyboard.

- **Keyboards.** Tap to open a separate Keyboards settings screen, where you can add or remove different international keyboards. Tap Add New Keyboard and then tap a keyboard to add one. To remove it, back up one screen by tapping the upper-left Keyboard button. Then tap the Edit button. Finally, tap the red delete icon next to the keyboard you don't want.

- **Shortcuts.** A shortcut is a set of characters that your iPhone will automatically replace for you when you type them. For example, you might prefer to say "I'm laughing out loud" instead of "lol" but want to save yourself from typing it out. This lists the current shortcuts you've set up. To add new ones, use the setting underneath this one, Add New Shortcut.

- **Add New Shortcut.** Use this control to add more shortcuts. Tap it and then enter the phrase (for example, "I'm laughing out loud") and the shortcut (for example, "lol"). To delete shortcuts, tap the Edit button on the main Keyboard settings screen and tap the red delete icon next to the shortcut you want to delete.

Getting Suggestions and Definitions

When you double-tap on a word, it is selected and a menu pops up. The menu options vary, but often you'll see Cut, Copy, and Paste, along with a right arrow **Ⓐ**. Tap the arrow to reveal two more options, Suggest and Define **Ⓐ**.

- **Suggest.** Tap Suggest to see a list of alternative spellings. If desired, tap one to change the word in your text field.

- **Define**: Choosing Define opens a built-in dictionary listing **Ⓑ**. Read about your word and press the Done button to return to your app.

> **TIP** The very first time you use the Define option, you'll be prompted to download the dictionary. You won't have to do it again.

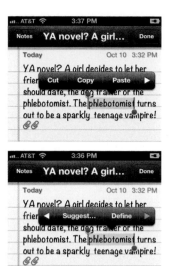

Ⓐ These are the options you'll see when you double-tap on an editable word. If you're looking at text that can't be edited (for example, a web page), you won't see all of these options.

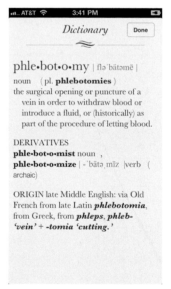

Ⓑ A dictionary listing for a word.

Searching

Over time, your iPhone is going to gather more and more data in the form of contacts, reminders, messages, music, videos, mail, and other things. Sometimes you'll want to find something but won't be quite sure where it is.

This is where your iPhone's ability to search through the things you've stored on it comes in handy.

To get to the iPhone's Spotlight Search screen, swipe the Home screen to the right until you reach it, or press the Home button from the first page of the Home screen. This opens the Spotlight Search screen Ⓐ.

When you search, you'll see results for a number of apps, identified by their icons Ⓑ. Tap on a result to open the app and see the matching content.

continues on next page

Ⓐ The Spotlight Search screen.

Ⓑ Spotlight Search results. You can tap one to see this result in its app, designated by the icon next to it.

You can control which apps are searched by opening Settings > General > Spotlight Search 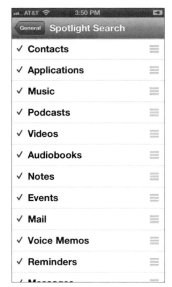. To remove an app from your search results, tap it to uncheck it. You can also change the order in which you see results by dragging the handles on the right and moving apps up and down.

Some apps allow you to search within them, which can be easier than using Spotlight Search. For example, if you're seeking a specific note you created in your Notes app, you may be better off searching within that app. To do so, open Notes and tap the status menu across the top, the bar at the very top with the current time displayed in it. This opens a search for content in the current app .

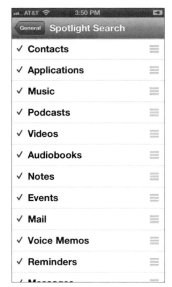

C Spotlight Search settings. Open this settings page by tapping Settings > General > Spotlight Search.

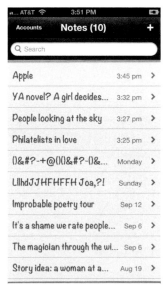

D Individual apps have their own search capabilities. To open the search box within the Notes app, tap on the status menu at the very top of the screen.

3

Setting Up
Your iPhone

So far you've taken it out of the box and learned what the buttons do, walked through the start-up screens, and learned to input and manipulate text with the online keyboard. But with that quick introduction, you haven't had a chance to start customizing your iPhone for yourself.

This chapter takes a look at lots of small (but important!) topics you need to know to make your iPhone your own, including things like protecting your iPhone with the addition of adding a passcode, customizing the Home screen, managing services that use your location, and locking your screen orientation.

In This Chapter

Setting a Passcode

Your passcode is a four-digit number or a more complicated password that you can set to help protect your iPhone from the eyes of other people. Once you set this code, you have to enter it to unlock your iPhone.

To set a four-digit passcode:

1. Tap Settings > General > Passcode Lock. This opens the Passcode Lock settings page **A**.

2. Tap Turn Passcode On. The Set Passcode screen slides up **B**.

3. Tap the numbers and set a four-digit passcode that you'll remember. (If you don't want to set one at this time, tap Cancel.)

4. Re-enter the same passcode once more. Your passcode is now set.

You can test the passcode you just set by pressing the Sleep/Wake button. You'll have to enter the passcode when you unlock the Lock screen **C**.

To turn off the passcode:

1. Tap Settings > General > Passcode Lock.

2. Enter your passcode.

3. Tap Turn Passcode Off.

4. Enter your passcode. Your passcode is now turned off.

A The Passcode Lock settings.

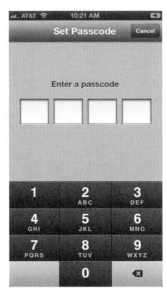

B This Set Passcode screen appears when you select Turn Passcode On.

C When you have a passcode set, you must enter it when you unlock your iPhone.

What If You Forget Your Passcode?

If you use a passcode, make sure it's one you remember, because there's no easy way to recover if you do forget. Odds are that you'll end up with an iPhone with none of your data on it.

If you've forgotten, you've got two options. One is that you can restore your iPhone by hooking it up to iTunes. This will strip all the data off it and then restore it to the last version you backed up.

Your other option is to go through and guess your passcode. You'd think, given that there are 9999 possibilities, that you could eventually stumble on it and all would be well. This is true, but after you guess incorrectly a few times, the iPhone increases a delay time before you can guess again. After a while, the delay time becomes absurdly long.

The moral of this story is that if you're going to use a passcode, make sure you won't forget it.

There's also the Erase Data setting. If this is set, after your 10 guesses your data is wiped from your iPhone, leaving restoring your iPhone your only option.

Additional passcode settings

The Passcode Lock screen **C** offers you a number of additional options:

- The Require Passcode option lets you set how long your iPhone can remain idle before you have to enter your passcode.

- Slide the Simple Passcode to Off if you want to lock your phone with a password, rather than a four-digit passcode. When you follow the steps to turn on your passcode, you'll see the QWERTY online keyboard rather than the numeric one and a text field. Just as with the four-digit code, make sure you don't forget it.

- When you've got your passcode protection on, you can use the next three controls on this screen to control what you can do without entering your code. You can choose Siri, Passbook app, and Reply with Message.

- When you turn on the Erase Data option, anyone who tries to sign in with the incorrect passcode will only get 10 tries before your iPhone erases your data.

- You can use your passcode to restrict specific apps. This means that to access one of these apps, you have to enter your passcode first. To manage which apps are restricted, choose Settings > General > Restrictions **D**. Tap Enable Restrictions. Any apps set to On will be restricted (read more on the Restrictions settings in Chapter 5, "Managing Your Settings").

D This screen allows you to restrict these individual apps from being used without your passcode being entered.

A This is the initial Home screen your iPhone displays. These apps can be reordered.

Customizing the Home Screen

When you first use your iPhone, you're presented with 17 icons for preinstalled apps on the Home screen **A**. It's not too bad (at first) to have these, but you'll almost certainly be adding apps to your iPhone over time, making things more crowded and disorganized.

Moving app icons

You can move icons around, and even move them to additional Home screens. Swipe right and left to see your additional Home screens.

To move app icons:

1. Touch and hold the app icon you wish to move.

2. When the icons begin to shake, drag the icon wherever you wish. (Be careful not to tap the black X on any app you've installed; doing so will delete it.)

3. Drag icons to the places you want them. If you want them between two other icons, drag them there and the other icons will shift to make room. If you want the icon on another Home screen, drag it to the right or left of your screen until the next Home screen appears.

continues on next page

4. Keep dragging icons until you're happy with their placement.

5. Press the Home button to finish.

> **TIP** Adding a new Home screen is as simple as dragging an app icon to the right edge of your screen until the new screen appears and then releasing it.

> **TIP** You aren't limited to moving apps around on the upper part of the screen. You can also drag icons in and out of the Dock at the bottom. For example, if you aren't interested in using the Music app, drag it up and out of the Dock and drag in an app you use more often.

Creating a folder

Not only can you move app icons, you can also organize them into folders. Each folder can hold up to 12 apps. To see how folders behave, take a look at the pre-created folder called Utilities.

Swipe the screen to the left and you'll see a Utilities folder. Tap on it to see the contents. Push the Home button to close the display of this folder's contents **B**. You can create and use your own folders as well.

B When you tap on a folder to see what apps it contains, the contents display beneath the folder.

Folder name text field

C When you create a folder in your Home screen, you can type a name in this text field. Your iPhone may suggest a name for you.

To create a folder:

1. Touch and hold an app icon you wish to place into a folder.

2. Drag the icon on top of any other icon. This tells your iPhone that you want to group these two apps together in a folder.

3. Release the icon and type the name of the folder you want to create in the text field that appears **C**. Your iPhone may already have a name in the field. You don't have to use it. Use the Delete key to erase it and type a new one if you wish.

4. When you're finished, press the Home button.

5. If you have any apps you'd like to add to this folder, follow the instructions on how to move icons, and then drag them over the folder icon.

To delete a folder:

1. Tap the folder icon you wish to delete.

2. Touch and hold an app icon inside the folder until the icons start to shake.

3. Drag the icon outside of the folder. Don't worry too much about where you drag it; you can always move it around later.

4. With the icons still shaking, tap the folder icon again.

5. Repeat with all icons in the folder. The folder will automatically be removed from your Home screen.

6. When you're finished, press the Home button.

Controlling Screen Orientation

Your iPhone can tell whether you're holding it upright (portrait) or sideways (landscape). Some apps don't turn (such as Weather and Game Center), and some do (for example, Mail, Safari, Camera). The Home screen never changes its orientation.

Locking the screen orientation

You can lock the iPhone so that it only uses portrait orientation.

To lock the screen orientation:

1. Double-click the Home button.

2. Swipe the dock at the bottom of the screen to the right. This displays media controls and a screen orientation lock button **A**.

3. Tap the screen orientation lock button on the left.

TIP When the orientation is locked, an icon appears in the status bar at the top of the screen.

A The Orientation button in the dock can be activated to force your iPhone to always use portrait orientation.

Ⓐ The Location Services screen lets you control whether or not your iPhone knows your location and which apps should have access to that information.

Setting Your Location

When you've turned on Location Services, your iPhone detects your location by using a built-in GPS device, Wi-Fi hotspots, and cell tower locations to get a fairly accurate idea of where you are. This information can be provided to various apps.

To turn on Location Services:

1. Open Settings > Privacy > Location Services **Ⓐ**.
2. Slide the Location Services control to On.

Managing Location Services

A variety of apps and services use your location to provide you with data.

To choose which apps are allowed to use your location:

1. Go to Settings > Privacy > Location Services **Ⓐ**.
2. Change the slider for any of the apps to On if you want it that app to use your location.

To choose which apps are allowed to know your location:

1. Go to Settings > Privacy > Location Services > System Services (at the bottom of the screen). This opens the System Services settings **B**.

2. Change the slider for any of the services to Off if you don't want that service to use your location.

3. At the bottom of this screen is a Status Bar Icon slider. When this is turned on, you'll see a purple arrow that indicates one of the listed services is using Location Services.

TIP Some apps and services in these lists have small arrows next to their slider controls. If the arrow is purple, the app or service is currently using **Location Services**. If it's gray, it has used **Location Services** in the past 24 hours.

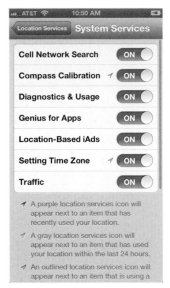

B These are the system services that use your location information.

Updating iOS

Apple regularly releases free updates and bug fixes for iOS. Some changes add features to iOS and the built-in apps, whereas others plug security holes or fix stability problems. You can update to the latest version of iOS over Wi-Fi.

Your iPhone uses the iOS operating system software. Apple periodically offers bug fixes and new versions of the iOS. These updates are free and can be performed on your iPhone without having to connect it to iTunes.

To check for and install updates to your iOS:

1. Plug your iPhone into a power source.

2. Set up a Wi-Fi connection (if you don't have one set up, see "Connecting to Wi-Fi" in Chapter 5).

3. Go to Settings > General > Software Update.

4. Your iPhone checks for available updates. If there aren't any, you'll see the message "Your software is up to date."

   If a new software version is available, follow the instructions on the screen to install it. You will now have the latest iOS software installed on your device.

TIP If you don't have Wi-Fi, you can still update your iPhone's iOS by connecting it to iTunes. Connect your iPhone to your computer and click on the Summary tab of iTunes.

Using Your iPhone as a Phone

Your iPhone is an amazing device, almost a notebook computer in your pocket. You can take photos with it, use it with FaceTime to have a video chat, use it as a personal assistant, keep track of your errands and events, check your email, browse the Web, play music, read books, play games, and carry out countless other activities with additional apps.

But don't forget, your iPhone is also a *telephone*. And not just a simple phone, but one that helps you, among other things, keep and organize your contacts, view records of calls you've made, manage numbers you call frequently, conduct calls with speakerphone and mute, and retrieve voicemail.

In this chapter, you'll take some time to discover just how your iPhone functions as a phone.

In This Chapter

Making Calls

Odds are you bought your iPhone on a multiyear contract with a cellular provider. If this is the case, your phone is likely ready to go.

TIP **If you don't yet have a carrier, you'll need to find one that supports the iPhone. For the most up-to-date information, visit the Apple support site and view carriers for your region (http://support.apple.com/kb/HT1937).**

Once your iPhone has been activated with a carrier, you can make calls.

To make a call:

1. Tap the Phone icon in your dock.

2. If the keypad is not visible, tap the Keypad button on the bottom of the screen **Ⓐ**.

   Dial using the keypad **Ⓐ**

   or

   tap and hold in the blue display area above the keypad to paste a number you've previously copied

   or

   use Siri or Voice Control to dial or call a contact (see Chapter 7, "Talking to Your iPhone").

3. If you make a mistake, tap the delete button to back up.

4. When your number appears in the blue area, tap Call.

To redial a number you just called:

1. Tap Keypad.

2. Tap Call to display the last number you dialed.

3. Tap Call again to place the call.

Ⓐ The iPhone's keypad.

Number display

Delete

Get your voicemail

Access the keypad (shown in this figure)

Access your favorite contacts to quickly call them

View a list of your contacts

See calls you've recently placed and received

TIP **If the number you entered is one that is stored in your Contacts app, the screen will display that contact's name and phone info under the number. (See Chapter 13, "Communicating," to learn more about managing your contacts.)**

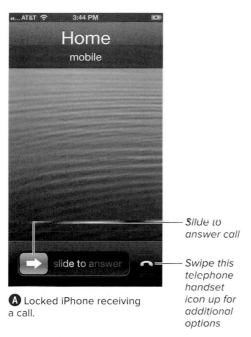

Slide to answer call

Swipe this telephone handset icon up for additional options

Ⓐ Locked iPhone receiving a call.

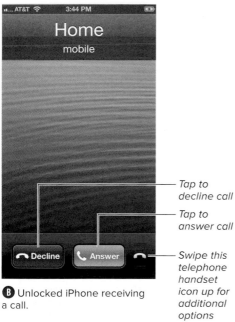

Tap to decline call

Tap to answer call

Swipe this telephone handset icon up for additional options

Ⓑ Unlocked iPhone receiving a call.

Getting Calls

You can, of course, answer incoming calls. But you can also send a call to your voicemail, silence a call, reply to a call with a text message, or remind yourself to return the call later. You can also turn on the Do Not Disturb feature, which sends unwanted calls to voicemail (see Chapter 6, "Handling Notifications," for more on using Do Not Disturb).

When your phone rings and it's locked, your screen will look like **Ⓐ**. When it's unlocked, you'll see **Ⓑ**.

To answer a call:

- If your iPhone is locked , slide the Slide to Answer control.
- If your iPhone is unlocked, tap the Answer button.

To send a call directly to voicemail:

- Quickly press Sleep/Wake (the button on top of your iPhone) twice.
- If you're using your EarBuds, press and hold the center button on the remote for a couple of seconds until you hear two beeps.
- If your phone is unlocked, tap the Decline button.

To silence a call:

- Press Sleep/Wake or either volume button. This silences the ringtone, but you can still answer the call.

To reply to a call with a text message:

1. Swipe the telephone handset icon upward.
2. Tap Reply with Message.
3. Tap the most appropriate item from the list of responses.

   You can choose: "I'll call you later," "I'm on my way," or "What's up?"

C Options revealed after you swipe the telephone handset icon upward when you receive a phone call.

To remind yourself to return a call:

1. Swipe the telephone handset icon upward .

2. Tap Remind Me Later .

3. Tap the most appropriate item from the list of responses: "In 1 hour," "When I leave," or "When I get home."

   These options use the Reminders app, and in the case of the last two, you need Location Services enabled (Switch on Settings > Privacy > Locations Services).

Change the Reply with Message

If you don't like the messages that appear when you choose the Reply with Messages option, you can edit them. Choose Settings > Phone > Reply with Message. Type over any of the fields to replace the existing messages .

D Reply with Message settings. Type over these default messages to customize them.

During a Call

While in the middle of a phone conversation, you can perform a variety of tasks. Sometimes you need to pull up the keyboard to enter numbers in response to an automated system. You can also use a speakerphone during your call, put the other caller on hold, or mute your side of the call.

If the iPhone's screen has faded to black during your call, move it away from your face 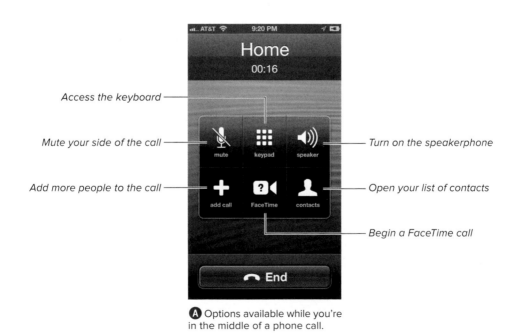. You'll end up on a screen with several options.

Actions you can take during a call include the following:

- The Mute button allows you to hear your caller while sounds coming from your end will not be broadcast to the person on the other end. The button turns blue when mute is on. Tap again to turn mute off.

- Tap the Keypad button to access the keyboard. Tap Hide Keyboard when you are done with it.

- Use the Speaker button to put the phone in speakerphone mode.

- The Add Call button allows you to add up to three more callers to your call for a total of five people. (See the task "To create a conference call" coming up in a moment.)

- Tap FaceTime to switch to a FaceTime call with the person on the other end, if they're also using a FaceTime-enabled device (see Chapter 13 for more on using FaceTime).

- Tap the Contacts button to view, and perhaps edit, the list of your saved contacts while you are in the call (read more about the Contacts app in Chapter 13).

Access the keyboard

Mute your side of the call

Turn on the speakerphone

Add more people to the call

Open your list of contacts

Begin a FaceTime call

A Options available while you're in the middle of a phone call.

B When you use the Add Call button, call a third party, and that person answers, the Add Call button changes to Merge Calls. Tap to begin your conference call.

To create a conference call:

1. While on a phone call, tap the Add Call button. This puts the person on the other end on hold temporarily.

2. Tap the Keypad button and enter another number

   or

   tap the Contacts button and choose a contact to call.

3. When the new caller answers, the Add Call button changes to say Merge Calls B. Tap this button. All of you are now on the same call.

4. Repeat the previous steps to add more callers.

TIP You can also start a conference call by using the Contacts button while you're talking to someone else. If you tap on a phone number in your contacts list, the first caller is put on hold and the second person is called. When that second person answers, you can press the Merge Calls button.

TIP See the Swap button in B? This shows up right before you tap Merge to create your conference. It appears whenever you are talking to someone and you have another person on hold. Tap the button to swap between the two callers—that is, put the person you are speaking with on hold while you speak to the caller who is currently on hold.

To remove someone from a conference call:

1. While in a conference call, tap the Conference banner across the top of the screen **C**. This opens a list of people on the conference **D**.

2. Tap the red icon to the left of the participant you wish to drop from the call.

3. The red icon changes to display the word *END*; tap it again.

4. Tap Back to return to the conference call screen.

To speak privately to one member of a conference call:

1. While in a conference call, tap the Conference banner on top of the screen **C**.

2. Tap the green PRIVATE button to the right of the participant you wish to speak with. Other participants will be placed on hold.

3. When you're finished, tap the Merge button to reinstate the conference.

TIP To add someone to your conference who is calling in, tap **Hold Call + Answer**, and then the **Merge Calls** button.

C Conference call screen.

D List of conference call participants.

Viewing Recent Calls

Every call you get is logged by your iPhone. This list can be helpful if you want to review who has called, see when someone called you, or easily save a caller's number in your contacts list. Not only can you see who has called you, you can also view a list of calls you've made and see when you made them.

To view recent calls:

1. Tap the Phone Icon in your dock.

2. Tap the Recents button at the bottom of the screen.

   This list shows you all calls you've received, all calls you've made, and all calls you've missed **A**. If the caller is in your contact list, you'll see that person's name. If not, the caller ID or phone number, if available, will be displayed.

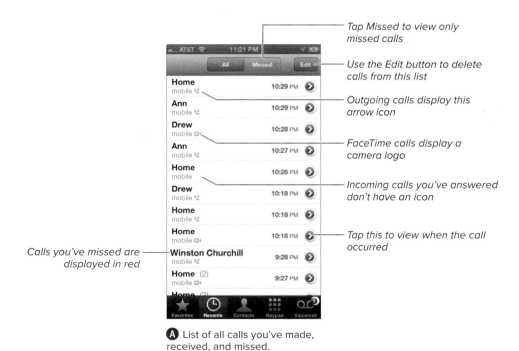

Tap Missed to view only missed calls

Use the Edit button to delete calls from this list

Outgoing calls display this arrow icon

FaceTime calls display a camera logo

Incoming calls you've answered don't have an icon

Tap this to view when the call occurred

Calls you've missed are displayed in red

A List of all calls you've made, received, and missed.

Recents Info Screen

When you tap the blue arrow to the right of a call in your Recents list, you'll see information about the call and caller, and several buttons to do things with this info 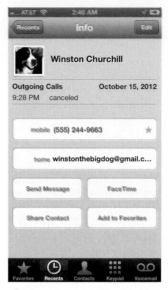 You can:

- Call the number back.

- Send a text message with the Message button.

- Tap FaceTime to initiate a FaceTime call.

- Add to Favorites. Tap this to designate this contact as a favorite so that it will appear in a list when you tap the Favorites button on the main Phone screen.

- If this call was from someone already in your contacts list, you can tap the Edit button and edit the listing (read more about editing contacts in Chapter 13).

Ⓑ Info screen for a call from your Recents list.

Setting Up Voicemail

The iPhone's voicemail is fairly simple to set up and use. Open it by going to Phone > Voicemail.

TIP If you have unheard voicemails, a badge will appear on the Voicemail icon telling you how many unheard messages you have.

Using the voicemail controls

Your main voicemail screen, **A**, lets you view all your messages, play your messages, access info on who called and when each message was left, set a greeting message, turn on a speaker while listening to messages, call the number back, and delete the call.

To set up your voicemail:

- If it's the first time you've opened your voicemail, you'll be prompted to enter a voicemail password and, if desired, record a greeting.

- You can change your password. Go to Settings > Phone > Change Voicemail Password.

- Enter a new greeting by tapping the Greeting button on the voicemail page. Tap Custom to record a new greeting.

- To add an alert sound that plays when you receive a new voicemail, go to Settings > Sounds > New Voicemail. Select a sound from the list.

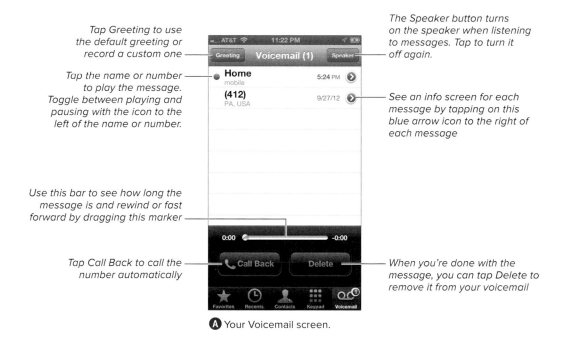

Tap Greeting to use the default greeting or record a custom one

Tap the name or number to play the message. Toggle between playing and pausing with the icon to the left of the name or number.

Use this bar to see how long the message is and rewind or fast forward by dragging this marker

Tap Call Back to call the number automatically

The Speaker button turns on the speaker when listening to messages. Tap to turn it off again.

See an info screen for each message by tapping on this blue arrow icon to the right of each message

When you're done with the message, you can tap Delete to remove it from your voicemail

A Your Voicemail screen.

Using Phone Settings

When you signed up with your cellular phone carrier, you probably ended up with some nice phone features like call forwarding or call waiting. The settings that work with these features are under Settings > Phone . Here's what these settings are for:

- **My Number.** Your iPhone's number is displayed here. You can change the number here, but changing it doesn't actually change it with your carrier; for the most part it simply changes anywhere on your iPhone where the number is displayed. It's best to leave it unchanged unless the carrier asks you to do so when you are changing numbers associated with the phone.

- **FaceTime.** You can toggle FaceTime capabilities on or off (read more about using FaceTime in Chapter 13).

- **Call Forwarding.** Tap it to see the slider to turn it on or off. If you turn it on, you will be presented with a screen where you can enter the number you wish your calls to be forwarded to.

- **Call Waiting.** Tap it to get to a slider where you can turn it on or off.

- **Show My Caller ID.** You can hide your caller ID by tapping this option and sliding it to off.

- **TTY.** This accessibility option can be used if you need to connect your iPhone to a TTY (a device that facilitates messaging for deaf and hearing-impaired users) with an adapter cable.

- **Change Voicemail Password.** If you need to change your voicemail password, tap this and enter your current code. Tap Done and enter a new password. Tap Done and enter your new password one more time.

Phone settings.

- **Dial Assist.** This option will automatically enter country codes for you when you're traveling in another country.

- **SIM PIN.** You can add a code or PIN number to lock your SIM module. This means that before a call can be made, the correct PIN has to be entered.

- **AT&T Services.** Depending on your location and carrier, you may see this option, which opens a list of shortcut codes you can contact for various services. Tapping on one of these will automatically dial the number, and some will send you a text message with information (with the exception of Directory Assistance). Tapping AT&T MyAccount opens a web page with more information.

Managing Your Settings

You might have already noticed how often you visit Settings. Every app on your iPhone has options you can control, and you'll find them under Settings.

In this chapter, you'll take a quick look at the status bar and the icons that appear in it that can be indicators of your current settings. Then you'll learn about some of the most commonly used settings for your iPhone, like wallpaper, screen brightness, and the iPhone Finder. Finally, this chapter covers everything you need to know about various network connects, including iCloud, iTunes, Wi-Fi, and VPNs, as well as pairing with Bluetooth devices.

Understanding the Settings

When you tap Settings, you're presented with a huge number of options. When you tap on each one, you see lots and lots more suboptions. Your settings are divided into sections. They are not named, but in general here's how they are organized.

- **Network:** Set up your Wi-Fi and Bluetooth, or disable them all when you get on an airplane **Ⓐ**.

- **Notifications:** Want to manage which apps can notify you and how? Want a break from being notified? Use this section **Ⓑ**.

- **General:** Control all the most basic, primary settings for your iPhone, things that affect all the other apps **Ⓒ**.

- **Primary Apple apps:** All the primary Apple apps that come installed on your iPhone have their settings here **Ⓓ**.

- **Media:** This section has settings for all the apps that let you buy and enjoy media **Ⓔ**.

- **Social media:** Manage Twitter and Facebook and how they interact with your iPhone apps **Ⓕ**.

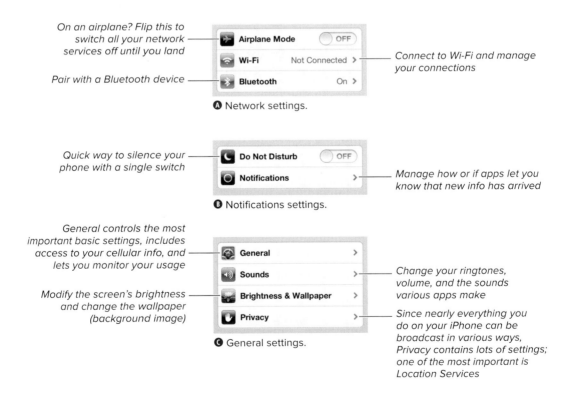

On an airplane? Flip this to switch all your network services off until you land

Pair with a Bluetooth device

Airplane Mode   OFF
Wi-Fi   Not Connected >
Bluetooth   On >

Connect to Wi-Fi and manage your connections

Ⓐ Network settings.

Quick way to silence your phone with a single switch

Do Not Disturb   OFF
Notifications   >

Manage how or if apps let you know that new info has arrived

Ⓑ Notifications settings.

General controls the most important basic settings, includes access to your cellular info, and lets you monitor your usage

Modify the screen's brightness and change the wallpaper (background image)

General   >
Sounds   >
Brightness & Wallpaper   >
Privacy   >

Change your ringtones, volume, and the sounds various apps make

Since nearly everything you do on your iPhone can be broadcast in various ways, Privacy contains lots of settings; one of the most important is Location Services

Ⓒ General settings.

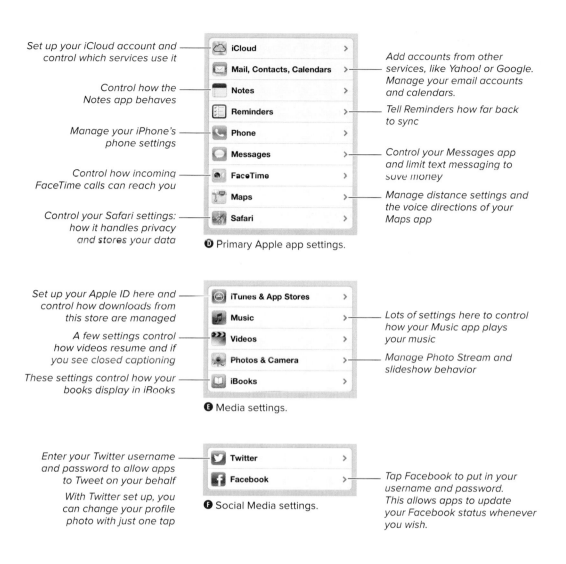

Set up your iCloud account and control which services use it

iCloud >

Add accounts from other services, like Yahoo! or Google. Manage your email accounts and calendars.

Mail, Contacts, Calendars >

Control how the Notes app behaves

Notes >

Reminders >

Tell Reminders how far back to sync

Manage your iPhone's phone settings

Phone >

Messages >

Control your Messages app and limit text messaging to save money

Control how incoming FaceTime calls can reach you

FaceTime >

Maps >

Manage distance settings and the voice directions of your Maps app

Control your Safari settings: how it handles privacy and stores your data

Safari >

❶ Primary Apple app settings.

Set up your Apple ID here and control how downloads from this store are managed

iTunes & App Stores >

Music >

Lots of settings here to control how your Music app plays your music

A few settings control how videos resume and if you see closed captioning

Videos >

Photos & Camera >

Manage Photo Stream and slideshow behavior

These settings control how your books display in iBooks

iBooks >

❷ Media settings.

Enter your Twitter username and password to allow apps to Tweet on your behalf

Twitter >

Facebook >

Tap Facebook to put in your username and password. This allows apps to update your Facebook status whenever you wish.

With Twitter set up, you can change your profile photo with just one tap

❸ Social Media settings.

Understanding the Status Bar

As you change your settings, you may notice a variety of icons in your status bar. These are useful for letting you see, at a glance, some of the services that are turned on in your settings.

TIP You'll also see some of these same icons in other places, not just in the status bar. Fortunately, the meanings remain the same. If you see the network activity icon on a settings page, for example, your iPhone is likely momentarily busy.

Status bar indicators

Cell Signal: You can tell the strength of your cellular signal by the number of bars.

Airplane Mode: This icon means both Wi-Fi and network connections are turned off. (See the sidebar "Airplane Mode.")

Wi-Fi: This icon indicates Wi-Fi is connected (see "Connecting to Wi-Fi").

4G **4G:** This icon indicates you're currently able to use 4G speeds on you cellular network.

Personal Hotspot: This icon indicates your phone can be used as a hotspot for Internet access. Many carriers let you sign up for an extra service that allows you to use your iPhone as a wireless hotspot for your other devices. Check with your cellular carrier for details.

Syncing: When you sync your iPhone with iTunes, you'll see this icon (see "Connecting with iTunes").

VPN **VPN:** This icon displays when you're connected to a virtual private network (see "Using VPNs").

Network Activity: This icon indicates that your iPhone is communicating with a network.

Call Forwarding: This icon indicates that call forwarding is on (see Chapter 4, "Using Your iPhone as a Phone").

Lock: This icon means your iPhone is locked.

Do Not Disturb: This icon means the Do Not Disturb setting is on (see Chapter 4.

Play: This icon appears when you are playing music on your iPhone.

Portrait Orientation Lock: When you lock the iPhone so the screen always remains in portrait orientation, you'll see this icon (see Chapter 3, "Setting Up Your iPhone").

Alarm: If you have an alarm set, you'll see this icon (see Chapter 14, "Maps, Weather, Stocks, and Clocks").

Location Services: This icon means that an app is currently using Location Services to pinpoint your position (see Chapter 3).

Bluetooth: When this icon is blue or white, your iPhone is linked to a Bluetooth device. If it's gray, Bluetooth is on but no devices are within range (see "Pairing with Bluetooth").

Battery: A battery icon with a lightning bolt means your iPhone is charging. When it's a battery with a plug icon, the battery is fully charged but still connected to a power supply. When your iPhone is not charging, the solid portion of the battery icon indicates how much power is left in the battery.

TIP You can use the Battery Percentage feature under Settings > General > Usage to see the remaining charge listed as a percentage to the left of the battery icon.

Bluetooth Battery: The remaining charge of a paired Bluetooth device will be displayed (see "Pairing with Bluetooth").

TTY: This icon indicates the iPhone is set up to work with a TTY machine used to translate spoken words into text for audibly impaired users.

Setting Up Find My iPhone

One of the most useful settings you can enable is the Find My iPhone feature. It uses Location Services and helps you find your phone when you've misplaced it. It also allows you to make your iPhone play a sound, remotely lock your phone with a passcode, or erase all your data if you choose. You can use another iPhone to take these actions, or you can browse to www.icloud.com.

To turn on Find My iPhone:

1. Go to Settings > Privacy > Location Services and make sure it's set to On.

2. On the same page, tap Find My iPhone. Slide the Find My iPhone control to On 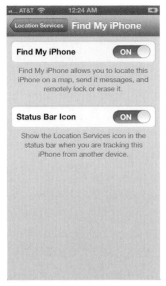.

3. Tap Allow on the confirmation screen that appears .

4. Optional: If you want the Location Services icon to appear in the status bar when you're using Find My iPhone on this phone, slide Status Bar Icon to On.

   If you worry about your iPhone being stolen, you might want to set this to Off so the culprit won't know you're looking for the iPhone. On the other hand, if anyone else knows your iCloud password, they can look for your iPhone. Setting this to On will give you a visual indicator that someone is looking at this iPhone's location on a map.

5. For Find My iPhone to work, you need to have your iCloud account set up. If you don't, see "Setting Up iCloud" later in this chapter.

Ⓐ Find My iPhone.

Ⓑ Confirmation screen for Find My iPhone.

C Find My iPhone in action, pinpointing the location with a green marker. Use the + zoom in control to better pinpoint the location.

D Click Devices to see a list of all of your devices that are using the Find My feature.

To use Find My iPhone:

1. Browse to www.icloud.com.

TIP In addition to going to the website, you have another option. You can also access the Find My iPhone functionality from another iPhone or iPad by downloading the Find My iPhone app. See Chapter 8, "Getting and Using New Apps," to find out how to install it.

2. Enter your Apple ID and password and click the arrow.

3. Click the Find My iPhone link.

   A map appears displaying the locations of all your devices with Find My Location services turned on **C**.

4. Click on Devices to see a list of your devices **D**. Select iPhone from this list.

continues on next page

5. A box appears with several options . You can choose to:

Play Sound: Your iPhone will play a sound for two minutes so you can find it.

Lost Mode: Putting your iPhone into lost mode will lock it with a passcode. Lost Mode also sends your iPhone a message displaying a contact number. Your iPhone tracks and reports its location to the Find My iPhone service.

Erase iPhone: This option will erase all information and media on your iPhone. Erase iPhone restores your iPhone to the original factory settings.

E After you click on a device, you see a list of options you can perform remotely.

Brightness and Wallpaper settings screen.

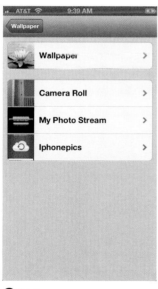

Ⓑ Wallpaper options.

Changing Wallpaper and Brightness

If you're tired of the default background design or wallpaper on your iPhone, you can change it to one of the included images or to one of your own.

The same settings page also lets you adjust the brightness of your screen. By default, your iPhone's screen brightness adjusts automatically depending on the ambient light. But you can override this behavior.

To change the wallpaper:

1. Choose Settings > Brightness & Wallpaper Ⓐ.

2. Tap the Wallpaper section of the screen Ⓑ. From this screen you can choose from among the following:

    Wallpaper: Tap to see thumbnails of wallpaper images you can choose from.

    Camera Roll: Tap to see thumbnails of images you've taken with your iPhone.

    My Photo Stream: Tap to see thumbnails of iCloud stored images you've taken with your iPhone and other Apple devices (see Chapter 12, "Creating").

    Other photo streams: If you've created custom photo streams, you'll see them listed here. For example, iphonepics is a custom photo stream.

    continues on next page

3. Tap one of the thumbnails from the sections listed in step 2 **C**.

   If you've chosen one of your own images, you can adjust the image. Use one finger to move the image, and two fingers in a pinch motion to zoom out, or spread to zoom in.

4. Tap the Set button. You may choose to change the Lock Screen, the Home Screen, or both **D**.

5. Tap one of these options. Your wallpaper has been changed.

To change the screen brightness:

1. Choose Settings > Brightness & Wallpaper **A**.

2. Drag the slider to the right or left to adjust brightness.

3. To keep your iPhone from automatically adjusting brightness, slide Auto-Brightness to Off.

C When you see Move and Scale, you can tap and drag the image to move, and pinch or spread two fingers to zoom in and out until you're happy with the displayed portion of the image.

D Choose the screens where you want the wallpaper to appear.

A Passcode entry screen for Restrictions settings.

B Restrictions settings enabled.

Managing Restrictions

If you're not the only one using your iPhone, and you want to restrict others from using certain features, you can add a passcode that has to be entered to gain access. You might want to keep some of your content private, prevent someone from making calls or buying apps, or protect a child from seeing inappropriate content. You can set restrictions to control these things.

To turn on restrictions:

1. Choose Settings > General > Restrictions.
2. Tap Enable Restrictions.
3. Enter a passcode **A**.
4. Re-enter the passcode.

With restrictions turned on, anyone trying to use restricted content or perform restricted activities will have to enter the passcode. You can restrict a variety of things from the Settings > General > Restrictions screen **B**.

Once you've turned on restrictions, you can use the Restrictions settings **B** to restrict access to apps, restrict access to some content based on rating, and restrict changes to content.

To restrict access to apps:

- In the Allow section **B**, drag any slider next to an app to On if you want restrictions to apply, or Off if you don't. You can also restrict Siri access and explicit language in this section.

To restrict access to content based on ratings:

- Scroll down to the Allowed Content section **C**. Tap Ratings For to choose which country's ratings to use. Tap each of the other items in this list and tap the appropriate rating level, which varies depending on content type. You can also restrict in-app purchases.

To restrict changes to content:

- Scroll down to the Privacy section **D**. Tap an item in this list and tap Don't Allow Changes **E** to restrict the content from being changed by other people and even other apps.

  When you set Don't Allow Changes, a tiny lock icon appears next to that listing in the main Restrictions screen.

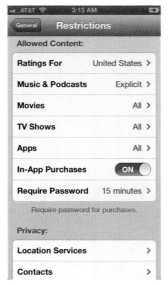

C Allowed Content section of Restrictions settings.

D Privacy section of Restrictions settings.

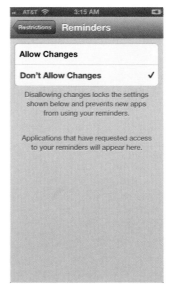

E Most of the apps listed in the Privacy section of the Restrictions settings let you set them to not allow any changes.

F Allow Changes and Game Center sections of Restrictions settings.

To restrict changes to accounts and volume limit:

- Scroll down to the Allow Changes section **F**. Tap an item in this list and tap Don't Allow Changes to keep accounts and maximum-allowed volume from being changed by other people.

To restrict access to Game Center:

- Scroll down to the Game Center section **F**. Move the slider to On to restrict access or Off to allow access to either multiplayer games or the ability to add friends to Game Center.

Setting Up iCloud

If you didn't set up an iCloud account when you worked through the iPhone setup process (see Chapter 2, "Touching Your iPhone"), you may want to. Your iCloud account lets you use the Find My iPhone feature, share Reminders and Calendar events between your Apple devices, and even sync your email everywhere. Your music, photos, contacts, and documents created with certain apps will also be stored and shared effortlessly. iCloud is built into your iPhone apps. It works in the background and sends and retrieves your data without you needing to do anything manually.

In addition to sharing your data with other Apple devices, you can get to your content by visiting www.icloud.com in a web browser.

Before you can use your iCloud account, you need to get an Apple ID if you don't already have one.

TIP **iCloud offers you 5 GB of storage for email, documents, and backups. Purchased music, apps, TV shows, and books, and photo streams don't count against this free space.**

To get a new Apple ID:

1. Go to Settings > iCloud and tap Get a Free Apple ID **A**. The Birthday screen opens.

2. Swipe the dials to enter your birth date **B**. Tap Next.

3. Enter your first and last name and tap Next.

4. Decide if you want to use a current email address or create a new iCloud email address. Tap Next.

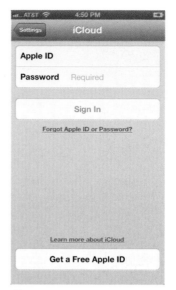

A iCloud Apple ID settings.

B Swipe the dials to enter your birth date.

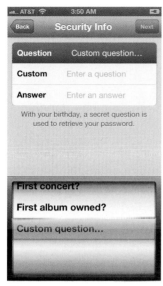

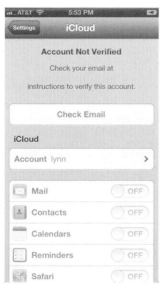

C You can create your own custom security question if you don't like any of the options.

D You still need to verify your account by visiting the inbox of the email address you entered in step 5 and responding to a verification email from Apple.

5. Either enter your current email address or create a new one with an icloud.com domain. Tap Next.

6. Enter a password, and then enter it again to verify. Tap Next.

7. Pick a security question by swiping the dial and type in an answer for it. You can also make up and enter your own question **C**. Tap Next.

8. Decide if you want to receive email updates from Apple. If not, slide the control to Off. Tap Next.

9. Read and review the Terms and Conditions. Tap Send by Email to get a copy sent to you. Tap Agree. A pop-up box asks you to tap Agree again.

10. Your account has been created but not yet verified **D**. You need to check your email by checking the email account you provided in step 5.

   In your email client, click on the link to Verify Now link to verify. This opens a login page. Use your Apple ID and password to verify.

To manage your iCloud account:

1. After you have an Apple ID or have created and verified it as in the previous steps, go to Settings > iCloud. This screen lets you choose which apps should sync with iCloud.

2. Use the sliders next to each app to decide if data from that app should be stored in iCloud for access on other Apple devices.

3. Turn iCloud Backup on if you want to store all your photos, documents, and settings. Keep in mind that this option can significantly increase the amount you're storing.

4. If you use a lot of data and want to increase your storage from the free 5 GB, tap Storage & Backup.

5. Tap Change Storage Plan to see more options you can purchase **E**.

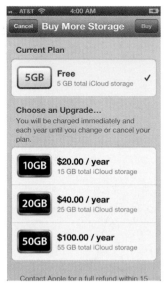

E If you plan on doing frequent backups through iCloud and loading your iPhone with lots of media, you may need to buy more iCloud space.

(A) iTunes with a connected iPhone.

Connecting with iTunes

Although you could get by without ever connecting your iPhone to your computer's iTunes software, there are definitely advantages to doing so. It allows you to easily pass data between your iPhone and your computer, including items like photos. It gives you an easy way to restore your iPhone should something go wrong or you need to replace your iPhone.

TIP To get the latest iTunes software for your computer, visit www.apple.com/itunes/download. iTunes is available for both Macintosh and Windows.

When you sync your iPhone with iTunes, your content is copied from your iPhone to your computer. If you've deleted something from your iPhone since the last time you synced, you can easily restore it to your iPhone.

To sync your iPhone with iTunes:

1. Connect your iPhone to your computer with the Lightning/USB cable.

2. The iTunes program on your computer should automatically begin. If it does not, start it manually.

3. In iTunes, click on your iPhone's name in the left-hand column **(A)**.

continues on next page

4. In the center pane of iTunes, click on each tab along the top of the pane **B**. You can customize syncing options for each.

5. When you're finished, click the Sync button in the bottom-right corner of iTunes.

TIP While your iPhone is syncing, it will say Sync in Progress. Don't disconnect it while it's syncing.

TIP If you ever want to restore a backup, connect your iPhone to your computer with the Lightning/USB cable. Right-click on your iPhone's name in the iTunes sidebar, and choose Restore from Backup.

Quite a few more options are available to you through iTunes. Though it's a good idea to consult an iTunes user guide, here's an overview of the options on the Summary tab **C**.

Sections on the Summary tab of iTunes include the following:

- iPhone **C**: The Summary tab displays your iPhone's name, its capacity, the software version it's running, its serial number, and your phone number.

- Version **C**: You can click Check for Update if you want to make sure there's no new version of your iPhone's iOS (operating system software). Also in this section is a button that lets you restore your iPhone to factory settings.

B Use the tabs at the top of the window to change syncing options for each media type.

C iPhone and Version sections of iTunes Summary tab.

D Backup and Options sections of iTunes Summary tab.

- Backup **D**: Contains options for backing up your data to iCloud or to your computer. Choose "Back up to this computer" if you don't want to use iCloud. You can also encrypt backups to your computer.

- Options **D**: You've got several choices. Three of them are worth mentioning here. First, you can make iTunes automatically open when you attach your iPhone's Lightning/USB cable. You can use Wi-Fi to sync, rather than having to connect your cable. And you can specify which songs and videos should be synced, rather than all of them.

Viewing Usage Info

All sorts of usage information is stored by your iPhone. This includes how much storage space is used by your apps and data, how much space you have left of your 5 GB of iCloud storage, and how much cellular data you've sent and received.

You can accomplish all these tasks under the Settings > General > Usage screen .

To view your iPhone's remaining storage:

- The Storage section displays how much space is available and how much each app and its data is consuming. Tap on an app name to see a further usage breakdown.

To view your iCloud remaining storage:

- The iCloud section displays your total storage and how much you've used. Tap Manage Storage to see a further breakdown and a link to purchase more storage if you need to.

To view your cellular usage:

- Choose Cellular Usage. This screen displays how much time you've spent in phone calls and how much cellular data you've sent and received.

  The data in the Cellular Network Data doesn't automatically reset every time you pay your bill. You need to tap Reset Statistics if you're trying to keep track of your data to avoid paying extra charges.

Ⓐ Usage Settings.

A Wi-Fi Settings.

Connecting to Wi-Fi

Your settings control which Wi-Fi network you are connected to or if you're connected at all. You can turn your Wi-Fi on or off. You can set your iPhone to automatically ask you if you want to join available networks. You can also view a list of available networks and connect to one. When you connect to a particular Wi-Fi network, your iPhone remembers and automatically connects to it whenever this network is in range. Sometimes you may not want to join a particular network you have joined in the past. You can make your iPhone forget a network so you can manually choose one to connect to.

You can accomplish all these tasks under the Settings > Wi-Fi screen **A**.

To turn your Wi-Fi on or off:

- Slide the Wi-Fi control to On or Off. When you turn off Wi-Fi, your only access to the network will be through your cellular data.

To be asked to join networks:

- Slide the Ask to Join Networks control to On. If your iPhone doesn't recognize any networks, it will ask you which you want to join.

To join a protected network:

- Under Choose a Network find the network you want to connect to. Protected networks require a password and are indicated by a lock icon. You must know the password. Tap it and then enter the password. Tap Join.

To join a closed network:

- Under Choose a Network, tap Other. You need to know the network name, password, and security type to connect. Enter this information. Tap Join.

To make your iPhone forget a network:

- Under Choose a Network find the network you want your iPhone to forget. Tap it and then tap Forget This Network.

TIP To adjust more network settings before connecting to a Wi-Fi network, tap the arrow next to a network. This screen allows you to set an HTTP proxy, define static network settings, or renew the settings provided by a DHCP server. Consult a network administrator for more information on the proper settings.

Airplane Mode

With your iPhone capable of making Wi-Fi, Cellular, and Bluetooth connections at the same time, you need a quick way to shut these down when you're about to take off in an airplane.

Tap Settings and switch the very first listing, Airplane Mode, to off.

Public Wi-Fi

More and more coffee shops, bookstores, and restaurants are offering patrons free Wi-Fi access. Often these networks don't require you to enter a password. Instead, after you connect, a screen will appear with a form asking you to agree to that establishment's terms of service. Generally, you just need to tap a check box and tap a button to proceed.

But be careful on these networks. Just as you appreciate the free service, so do hackers with an eye to getting your passwords, login information on various websites, and your private data.

A VPN Settings.

Using VPNs

A *virtual private network* (VPN) is an encrypted network protocol often used by companies to let employees from remote locations gain access to the company's internal network. VPNs work over both Wi-Fi and cellular data network connections.

To set up and use a VPN:

1. Choose Settings > General > VPN **A**.

2. Slide VPN to On. The Add Configuration screen appears. If it doesn't, tap Add Configuration.

3. Use the information provided to you by your network administrator to enter the proper settings. Tap Save.

4. If you need more than one VPN configuration, repeat steps 1–3.

Pairing with Bluetooth

You can pair Bluetooth devices, such as a keyboard, with your iPhone.

To pair a Bluetooth device with your iPhone:

1. Put your device in pairing mode. This will vary by device; see the manufacturer's instructions.

2. Choose Settings > Bluetooth. Your iPhone immediately begins searching for the device.

3. When your iPhone finds the device, a name appears in the Devices list.

4. Tap the appropriate device and follow the instructions (these will vary depending on the type of device it is).

TIP **If you ever need to unpair a device, tap on the blue icon and tap Forget This Device. Then tap the confirmation.**

6

Handling Notifications

Most apps that receive new data or deal with time-sensitive information want to let you know. That's what notifications are for. They're little messages appearing on your screen to tell you what's new. You can tap on a notification to go to the appropriate app and manage the data.

Lots of apps want to send you notifications. While you might want some of them, you can modify your iPhone's settings to only get the notifications from the apps you want. You can also adjust the style of notification you receive.

Notification Center lets you quickly get at things like your local weather, stock reports, and your upcoming appointments. You'll find out how to manage your notifications, control what kind of notifications you get, and use Notification Center in this chapter.

In This Chapter

Getting Notifications

Many of your apps want to display, or "push," notifications to you when events occur or new data arrives. These notifications will display on your iPhone whether or not you're using the app at the time. You can control which apps can send you notifications with the Notifications settings.

Notification styles

Notifications come in two different styles:

- **Alerts.** An alert is a window that requires you to take an action by tapping on it to get rid of it .

- **Banners.** A banner is a short bit of text with an app's icon. It shows up on top of the iPhone screen and then goes away on its own **B**.

  You can also add a sound effect or ringtone to each notification.

You can control the type of notification you get in the notification settings (see the task "To change the style of notification for an app" in the next section).

A A notification alert. You have to tap either the Close or View button to dismiss this alert. The View button will open the app that generated this notification.

B A notification banner. This banner will disappear after a few seconds.

C The Notifications settings display a list of apps that can be configured to send you notifications or to appear in Notification Center (discussed later in this chapter).

Apps with Notifications

Not all of the apps that come preinstalled on your iPhone offer alerts, banners, and sound notifications. Here are the ones that do:

- Phone
- Messages
- Passbook
- Reminders
- Photos
- Game Center
- Calendars

Other apps, such as Weather and Stocks, stream information but don't offer you alerts, banners, or sounds.

Additional apps you install (see Chapter 8, "Getting and Using New Apps") may also have notifications. If they do, they'll appear in the Notifications settings **C**.

Customizing Notifications

Notifications are meant to make your life easier, and, as such, they have a number of settings so you can make them as useful as possible. For example, you can choose which apps send them out, you can change the style of notification on a per-app basis, and you can give them sounds.

To turn off notifications for an app:

1. Open Settings > Notifications to access the Notifications settings **A**.

2. Slide down to the app you're looking for and tap it. (It may be in the In Notification Center section or below it in the Not in Notification Center section. Check out "Managing Notification Center" later in this chapter for more about these sections.) This opens the Notifications settings for just that app.

3. To turn off alerts or banners, tap the None option under Alert Style **B**.

4. There may also be a sound when a new notification event occurs. The setting that controls this varies depending on the app; for example, it might be called Sounds, Text Tone, Ringtone, or Reminder Alerts.

To change the style of notification for an app:

1. Open Settings > Notifications to access the Notifications settings **A**.

2. Slide down to the app you're looking for and tap it.

3. Tap either Banners or Alerts under the Alert Style **B**.

A The Notifications settings.

B Notifications settings for a particular app, including the Alert Style setting.

C When turned on in an app's Notification settings, red badges display on that app's icon in the Home screen. The number in the badge indicates how many new notifications for that app have arrived since the last time you opened it. In this case, one new reminder is waiting for you in the Reminders app.

As you look through the Notifications settings for each app, you'll notice a number of different options, depending on the app. Here are a few of the most common ones and what they do:

- **Notification Center.** Controls whether the app appears in your Notification Center (discussed later in this chapter).

- **Show.** Specifies how many of the most recent notifications will appear in Notification Center. Your options are 1, 5, or 10.

- **Alert Style.** Sets your alert style to banners, alerts, or neither.

- **Badge App Icon.** Controls whether to display a red badge on the app's icon in the Home screen. This badge displays a number that represents how many new notifications have arrived since you last used the app **C**.

- **View in Lock Screen.** When this setting is enabled, your alert or banner will show up on the lock screen when your iPhone is locked.

- **Sounds.** Sounds associated with various apps' notifications may have different names. Some sound controls, such as the ringtone for the Phone app, let you pick a sound. Others only allow you to turn the sound on or off.

TIP When you're in the Notifications settings, each app lists what kind of notifications it currently sends you in gray text under its listing. You can tell at a glance if badges, alerts, sounds, and banners are enabled for a given app.

Using Do Not Disturb

Suppose you don't want to receive sounds related to notifications or ringing from phone calls for an hour, or maybe you want all sounds to cease except for specific phone calls. You can control this with the Do Not Disturb settings. When activated, this feature silences calls and sounds from notifications, although you will still receive any alarms you have set up.

To turn off notifications indefinitely:

1. Choose Settings.
2. Slide the Do Not Disturb control to On. You won't be interrupted by any phone calls or notifications until you slide the control back to On.

To turn off notifications for a specific amount of time:

1. Choose Settings > Notifications > Do Not Disturb to access the Do Not Disturb settings 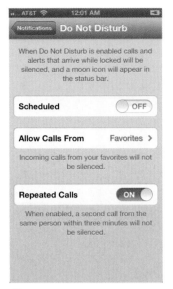.
2. Slide Scheduled to On. From and To settings appear.
3. Tap the From and To settings to open the Quiet Hours screen .

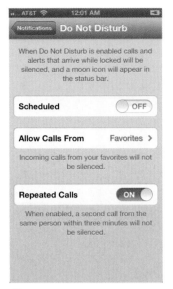

Ⓐ The Do Not Disturb settings.

Ⓑ Tap either From or To and use the dials to set the time to begin and the time to end the Do Not Disturb period.

C Use the Allow Calls From options to specify who can call you when you have Do Not Disturb switched on.

4. Slide the dials to set the From and To times. From is the time you want to turn off all notifications, and To is when you want them to resume. You're limited to turning notifications off only up to 24 hours from the current time. They'll automatically return when the To time is reached.

5. When you're done, tap Do Not Disturb to return to the previous screen.

TIP A quick way to tell if your Do Not Disturb is active is to look at the top bar on your unlocked screen, the status bar. You should see a small crescent moon symbol ☾.

To allow specific calls when Do Not Disturb is on:

1. Choose Settings > Notifications > Do Not Disturb.

2. Tap Allow Calls From. The Allow Calls From screen appears **C**.

3. Choose from the options Everyone, No One, or Favorites. If you have Groups set up in your Contacts app, you can select specific groups to allow through (see Chapter 4, "Using Your iPhone as a Phone," for more on setting Favorites and creating groups in your Contacts).

4. Tap the Do Not Disturb button to return to the previous screen.

TIP If you've decided not to allow any calls through but you still want some people to be able to reach you, you can set Settings > Notifications > Do Not Disturb > Repeated Calls to On. For those you want to get through despite the Do Not Disturb setting, tell them that your phone will ring if they call twice within three minutes.

Managing Notification Center

Notification Center is a handy screen on your iPhone that lets you see at a glance all your most recent notifications, such as email subjects, reminders, calendar events, Twitter messages to you, and text messages. You can also monitor the weather and the stock market and easily post to Twitter or Facebook from this screen. You can see an example of Notification Center with information, including weather, stock market data, calendar events, and reminders in .

TIP If you miss what a banner says before it goes away, don't fret. Simply open Notification Center to see the notifications you've received most recently.

A Notification Center, with weather, stocks, Twitter and Facebook posting buttons, reminders, and calendar events.

To access Notification Center:

1. Unlock your iPhone.

2. Tap, hold, and swipe downward from the status bar at the very top of the screen. This opens the Notification Center screen.

B Drag the handle to the right of any app to move it up or down in the list. The app at the top of the list appears first on the Notification Center screen.

To change the order of notifications in Notification Center:

1. Choose Settings > Notifications.

2. Under Sort Apps, tap Manually.

3. Tap the Edit button in the top right.

4. Tap and drag the handle to the right of any apps in the list and move the app up or down **B**.

5. Tap the Done button when you're finished.

> **TIP** If you tap By Time under Settings > Notifications > Sort Apps, the notifications on your Notification Center will always be ordered by the most recent one you received. For example, if you just got a message, the Message app's notifications will appear at the top of the screen.

Adding or removing Notification Center apps

There are two ways to add or remove apps:

■ Under each app's settings under Settings > Notifications, locate and tap the app you wish to add or remove. Slide the Notification Center control to the appropriate setting.

■ Follow the previous steps to change the order of apps in the Notification Center, and drag any apps you do not wish to appear to the very bottom of the list, under the section called Not in Notification Center.

Talking to Your iPhone

Have you talked to your iPhone lately? If you've made any phone calls, you've spoken into it. But talking directly to your iPhone gives you access to a few powerful and timesaving features you ought to know about.

This chapter is all about talking to your iPhone. You'll learn how to create voice memos for yourself, and, the most interesting thing of all, how to use your personal assistant, Siri, to do and find all kinds of things for you.

Creating Voice Memos

You can use your iPhone's Voice Memos app to record audio and play it back later. It can be recorded using the built-in microphone (the same way that you talk to people during phone calls) or through a microphone built in the EarPods that came with your iPhone.

To record a voice memo:

1. Open Voice Memos by tapping the Utilities Folder and tapping Voice Memos .

2. Practice talking and notice the needle in the VU meter on the bottom of the app **B**.

   If the needle moves, your iPhone is picking up your voice. It only needs to reach around 10 to be loud enough.

A The Voice Memos app is stored in the Utilities folder. Tap the folder, and then tap Voice Memos.

Tap to play

Tap to view list of saved memos

B Voice Memos recording screen.

Tap to finish recording

Tap to pause

C Voice Memos screen while recording.

3. When you're ready, tap the red record button to the left of the meter. Begin speaking.

   As you speak, a red banner appears across the top of the app to let you know the app is recording **C**.

4. You can pause your recording by tapping the red button. Tap it again to restart.

5. When you're done, tap the black stop button to the right of the meter. Your recording has been saved.

To view your recorded voice memos:

- Access your saved voice memos by tapping the silver list button to the right of the meter. This opens a list of your memos **D**.

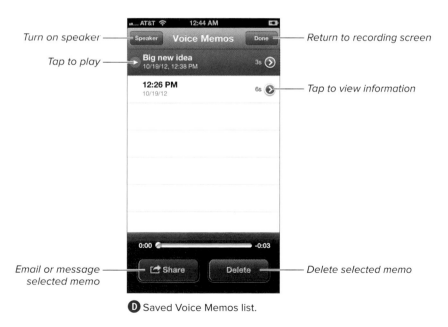

Turn on speaker

Tap to play

Email or message selected memo

Return to recording screen

Tap to view information

Delete selected memo

D Saved Voice Memos list.

To manage your recorded voice memos:

- To play a memo, tap it. Tap it once more to pause.

- Tap and drag the playhead on the timeline at the bottom of the app to jump from point to point in the memo.

- Delete a memo by tapping on it to select it and then tapping Delete.

- Share a memo by selecting a memo and tapping the Share button. Tap either Email or Message to send your voice memo as an audio M4A file to a recipient.

To trim a voice memo:

1. You can trim, that is delete, part of a voice memo. From the Voice Memos list screen **D**, tap the blue icon to the right of the memo you want to trim. This opens an info screen for this memo **E**.

2. Tap the trim button, and drag the handles on either end of the yellow trim bar to remove part of the recording.

3. You can test the recording by tapping the play button to the left. When you're happy, tap Trim Voice Memo.

TIP If you tap the name of your memo while you are in the info screen, you can give it a new name, or label. Tap on the name and a label screen appears. Choose one of the existing ones, or tap Custom and enter your own name for the recording.

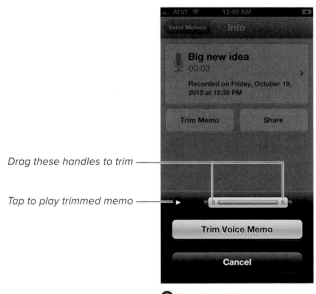

Drag these handles to trim ———

Tap to play trimmed memo ———

E Trim Voice Memo.

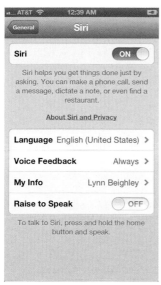

Ⓐ Siri settings.

Ⓑ Passcode Lock screen with passcode turned on and Siri set to *No*.

Configuring Siri

Siri is your voice-controlled personal assistant. With Siri, you can ask your iPhone for all sorts of information or perform a function and it will do its best to provide you with an answer or accomplish the task using the Internet, iCloud, and the apps installed on your iPhone.

You first need to enable it, and then you may wish to change some of Siri's default settings.

To enable Siri:

- Go to Settings > General > Siri **Ⓐ**. Slide the Siri control to On.

To keep Siri from operating from the lock screen:

1. This is accomplished by adding a passcode to unlock your iPhone. Go to Settings > General > Passcode Lock **Ⓑ**.

2. Tap Turn Passcode On and enter a passcode.

3. Confirm the passcode.

4. On the Passcode Lock screen, slide Siri to Off.

continues on next page

Configuration options on the Siri settings screen Ⓐ include the following:

- **Siri:** Turns Siri On or Off.

- **Language:** Tap this to change the language or language dialect Siri speaks in.

- **Voice Feedback:** Choose whether Siri will respond to you vocally. When you tap Voice Feedback, you can choose Handsfree Only or Always. Handsfree Only will make Siri talk only when you're using EarPods, headphones, or Bluetooth audio. Always means that Siri will always talk.

- **My Info:** Tap this option to choose your contact entry from Contacts, which gives Siri access to this information about you.

- **Raise to Speak:** If you turn this option on, every time you put the iPhone to your ear, Siri will activate. Leave this off to use the Home button to activate Siri.

A Siri's input screen.

Talking to Siri

If you've turned Siri on in your Settings, you can start using it for all kinds of tasks and requests for information.

To talk to Siri:

1. Press and hold the Home button or press and hold the center button on your EarPods. The Voice Control screen appears **A** and your iPhone makes a double chime.

2. Speak your request. When you stop, Siri will chime and analyze your request for a split second.

3. Siri will then return with a response.

Here's a sampling of things you can ask Siri to do:

- Call someone in your contacts: "Call Elizabeth."

- Dictate an email and send it to a contact: "Email Brian."

- Make a reservation: "Make a reservation at La Froufrou tonight."

- Play movie trailers: "Show The Hobbit trailer."

- Make a Facebook post or tweet to Twitter: "Send tweet."

- Launch an app: "Open Notes."

- Set a reminder: "Remind me to buy dog food at noon."

- Send a text: "Text Cynthia."

- Schedule a meeting: "Meet with Professor Brown at three today."

- Set an alarm. "Wake me up at 7 am."

- Set a timer. "Set a timer for 25 minutes."

Here's a sampling of things you can ask Siri to find out:

- Find a contact: "Find Angela Drake."

- Get directions to an address: "Get directions to 235 Main Street."

- Get show times, movie facts, and movie reviews: "Get show times for The Hobbit."

- Find a restaurant, read reviews: "Find pizza."

- Find sports scores, schedules, and stats: "When do the Eagles play?"

- Ask informational questions that Siri can search for: "How many calories in an apple?"

- Check the weather: "What's the weather today in London?"

- Track stocks: "Boeing."

TIP Siri can do other things that haven't been mentioned here, and its capabilities continue to increase. You can get an overview of what Siri can do by asking Siri the question, "What can you do?"

Using Voice Control

Voice Control steps in when Siri is not activated. You can use Voice Control to make phone calls and play music with voice commands. (You can also do these things by speaking to Siri, but it's useful to know about Voice Control when you are without Internet access or if you have Siri switched off.) Voice Control operates in basically the same way Siri does and uses the same voice, but it is limited to those two tasks.

To use Voice Control, hold the Home button until it activates, and then say something like "Call Dan Jones at home." If Dan is in your address book with a home number listed, your iPhone will call it. You can also tell it to call a number by speaking the digits. For example, "dial five five five one two one three."

Getting and Using New Apps

Your iPhone comes with some good apps, but with literally hundreds of thousands more that you can add, you'll certainly find some that make your life easier or more fun.

This chapter is all about getting new apps, how to find them, how to install them, and how to configure them.

In This Chapter

Setting Up Your Apple Account

When you want new apps, the way to get them is to open the App Store app. But before you can install any new apps, you have to provide Apple with information on how you will pay for any apps with a purchase price. Unfortunately, this applies whether or not the app is free.

To add payment information to your Apple ID:

1. Go to Settings > iTunes & App Stores 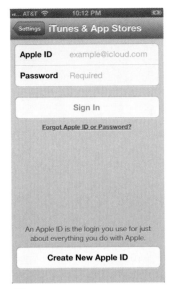. Your Apple ID should be in the blank; if not, enter it and your password. Tap Sign In.

2. You'll see a message that your Apple ID has not been used in the iTunes store. Tap Review.

3. For Account Settings, choose the correct country and tap Next.

4. Read the terms and conditions and tap Agree. Confirm by tapping Agree again.

5. The next screen is the Account Settings screen 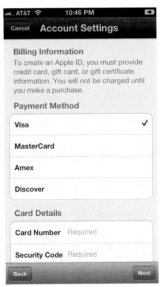. It requires you to select a credit card type and enter a card number, security code, expiration date, billing address, and phone. Enter this information and tap Next.

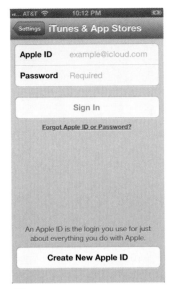

Ⓐ iTunes & App Stores settings screen.

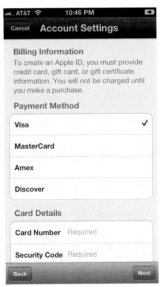

Ⓑ Account Settings for your Apple ID account.

Finding Apps

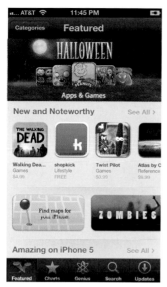

 The App Store is an app on your iPhone that lets you find, install, and update apps. There are both free apps and ones you have to pay for. When you've associated credit card information with your Apple ID, you can easily purchase apps directly from the App Store with a single click.

Tap the App Store icon on the Home Screen to open it. The App Store **A** has five main sections accessible by tapping the icons in the toolbar at the bottom of the app. These are, from left to right, Featured, Charts, Genius, Search, and Updates.

A Featured displays a variety of new and recommended apps.

TIP The Categories button on the top of the Featured and Charts screens allows you to filter the apps to just one category. Or tap All Categories to see all app categories.

Understanding Apps

When you hear the word *app*, think software or computer program. Your iPhone arrived with a number of preinstalled apps, developed by Apple. (One of these apps is, ironically, the App Store where you can find and download new apps.) Apps you find in the App Store are almost all the work of third-party developers. These developers have to go through an Apple approval process, which means you can have confidence in these in apps.

Sometimes Apple removes an app from the store if it's buggy or in some other way violates Apple's policies. When it's removed from the store, it won't be removed from your iPhone. You may want to take a peek and see if your installed apps are still offered at the App Store once in a while.

Featured

- The Featured screen 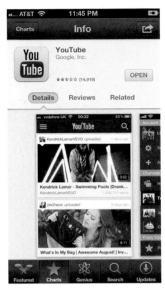 has several sections that may vary depending on what Apple is trying to promote. New and Noteworthy and What's Hot (the most downloaded apps) are standard.

- Under each section is a set of recommended apps. Each of these apps displays the name, category, and cost. Swipe to the left to see more apps.

- Each section has a See All link that you can tap to view all the recommended apps, and more recommendations, in a list.

- Scroll down to the bottom of the app to see the Redeem and Apple ID buttons. If you have a gift card, tap to enter and redeem it. The Apple ID button should display your Apple ID. If it doesn't, tap it and enter the requested information.

- When you tap on an app icon, you see an information screen where you can see the app's rating, read more about the app, view screen shots, read user reviews, and purchase the app .

B Info screen for an app.

Charts

- The Charts screen **C** displays the most popular apps. The three sections are Paid, Free, and Top Grossing. Swipe to the left to see more apps, or tap See All to see a list view.

Genius

- Genius **D** gives you a list of 15 apps recommended to you based on previous apps you've purchased from the App Store. Swipe to the left to see them.

- If you switch Genius on, you have to enter your Apple ID password and agree to the terms of service.

C Charts displays the most popular apps.

D Genius offers suggestions based on your past app purchases.

Clear search box

E Search for apps.

- Tap the Not Interested button at the bottom of an app if you aren't interested. This will help fine-tune your list.

Search

- Search **E** is exactly that, a search box. Tap to type in a name or keyword for an app. For example, you might want to find a cooking app with recipes. Start typing recipes, and as you type, a list of suggestions appears.

- Tap any of the results to see a set of apps fitting your search. Swipe to the left to see more.

- Clear the search box by tapping the X icon to the right.

Updates

- Developers of apps often need to release new versions to offer bug fixes or new features. Any apps you've purchased and installed will show up here when there's a new release. All you need to do is tap to update, or if you have several, tap Update All.

- When updates are available, the Update icon at the bottom of the App Store will display a badge, a red circle with a number. This number indicates how many updates are available. This badge also appears on the App Store icon on the Home screen.

- When you tap Update, the App Store closes and you see the app icon on the Home screen with a progress bar beneath it.

- Some apps may require you to be connected via Wi-Fi to update.

Getting and Deleting Apps

When you find an app you may want, you should take a look at its info screen and then, if you're sure, install it.

To view an app's Info screen:

- Tapping on an app icon anywhere in the App Store will open an Info screen  for that app.

- Everything you ever wanted to know about this app is on its Info screen. This includes the developer's name, a star rating based on user reviews, a price button that you tap to purchase the app, a description and screen shots of the app, contact information for the developer, posting date, version, size, and age-appropriate rating. There's also a link to reviews and a link to a list of related apps.

- Tap the arrow button on the top right to open a menu of sharing options **B**. These options allow you to send out a link to the app via email, text message, Twitter, or Facebook. You an also copy the link.

A App Info screen.
Sharing options

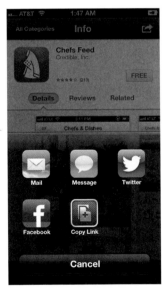

B Sharing options on the app Info screen.

To purchase and install an app:

1. In the app's info Ⓐ screen in the App Store, tap on the button with a price on it (or FREE if it's free). The button turns green and says BUY APP.

TIP After tapping BUY APP, you may be prompted for your Apple ID and password, or just the password. You may also have to agree to new Apple App Store terms and conditions. These change pretty frequently.

2. Tap again to make the purchase and have the app automatically install on your iPhone.

3. The icon appears on your Home screen while it's installing, and the progress bar goes away when it's done.

TIP Newly installed apps are marked with the word NEW until you open them for the first time.

4. You can pause the download by tapping its icon. To resume downloading, tap the icon again.

Managing App Settings

There's no one place to find settings for third-party apps. They may have buttons or links called Tools, Options, or Settings.

Some apps do install their settings in the Settings app. To check and change settings for an App Store app, open Settings and scroll down the page looking for the icon associated with the app. If it's there, tap on it to reach its settings.

To delete an app:

1. Locate the icon of the app you wish to delete in the Home screen.

2. Tap and hold the icon until all the icons begin to wiggle.

3. Tap the small x in the corner of the app.

4. Choose Delete in the confirmation alert that opens. Tap Delete.

5. Press the Home button.

Updating Apps

When you see a red badge on the App Store icon in the Home screen or on the Updates icon in the App Store, that means at least one of your apps has an update available.

To update apps:

1. In App Store, tap Updates in the bottom toolbar. A list of apps with available updates appears.

2. To update an app, tap the Free button next to its name.

   or

   To update everything in the list with a single tap, tap Update All.

3. Enter your Apple ID and password or password, if requested, and then tap OK.

TIP **Progress meters appear on the Home-screen icons of the apps being updated. When the download completes, updates are installed immediately.**

To reinstall an app:

1. In App Store, tap Updates.

2. Tap Purchased to see a list of apps you've ever purchased for any iPhone. Tap "Not on this iPhone" to see apps you've purchased but that are not installed on this iPhone.

3. Find the app in the list and then tap the button or iCloud button to the right of its name.

Reading, Listening, and Watching

You know you can listen to music on your iPhone, but you can also browse the web, read newspapers and books, and watch movies.

While you're waiting at the DMV, you can use Safari, the iPhone's native web browser. Or you can catch up on the headlines with Newsstand. If you'd prefer, you can pick up where you left off in that novel you've been reading on iBooks. Buy some new music on iTunes and listen to it immediately. Or rent a movie, plug in your EarPods, and watch it until your number is called.

In This Chapter

Browsing with Safari

 Safari is your iPhone's built-in web browser. With it, you can view web pages (with the exception of embedded Adobe Flash movies, which Safari doesn't support).

The Safari app  lets you type in URLs (web addresses), search the web, go back and forth between pages, navigate pages by tapping links, share URLs in a variety of ways, print web pages, bookmark web pages, save pages to your reading list to read offline, and more.

Reload this page

Address bar

Search box

Tap a link to browse to it. Or tap and hold a link to see more options.

Double-tap or spread your thumb and finger to zoom in. Double-tap again or pinch to zoom out.

Windows button lets you view other open web pages or open a new Safari window. Seven windows are currently open.

Previous page you viewed

Next page

View your reading list, history, and bookmarks

Actions button opens controls for sharing and performing other actions

A The Safari app.

Open Safari by tapping the Safari icon in the dock. Then start exploring:

■ Tap the actions button in the center of the bottom menu to open a set of page options **B**.

continues on next page

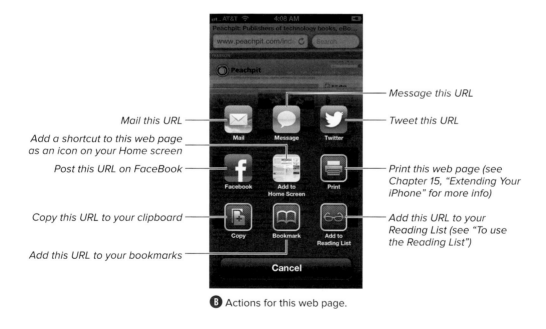

Mail this URL

Add a shortcut to this web page as an icon on your Home screen

Post this URL on FaceBook

Copy this URL to your clipboard

Add this URL to your bookmarks

Message this URL

Tweet this URL

Print this web page (see Chapter 15, "Extending Your iPhone" for more info)

Add this URL to your Reading List (see "To use the Reading List")

B Actions for this web page.

- Tap and hold a link and additional options related to the link roll up **C**.

- To open a new browser window, tap the window button. Swipe through currently open windows, close them by tapping the red x icon, or open a new browser window by tapping New Page **D**.

- To browse to a website, tap in the address bar and type in a URL. Then tap the blue Go button.

TIP If the URL ends in something other than .com, like .org or .net, tap and hold the .com button on the keyboard. A menu will appear. Move your finger to the correct choice and release.

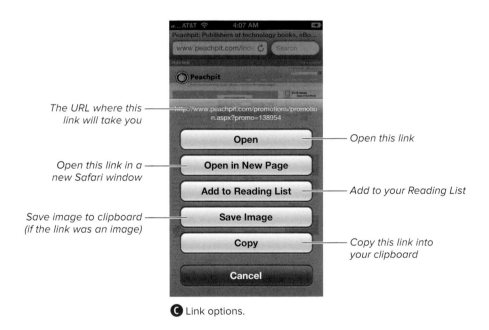

The URL where this link will take you

Open this link in a new Safari window

Save image to clipboard (if the link was an image)

Open this link

Add to your Reading List

Copy this link into your clipboard

C Link options.

- To search the web, tap in the search box and type, and then tap the blue Search button.

- To search for text in the current page, tap and enter the text in the search box. Scroll down to the bottom of the list of matches to the On This Page section and tap that result.

TIP Web pages can sometimes be easier to view if you turn your iPhone on its side (landscape).

TIP Although reading a web page on the small screen of your iPhone is not ideal, you can zoom in to make viewing easier. Double-tap on text or an image in the page to make the page a little larger. Or to really zoom in, use your thumb and index finger and spread them apart. Pinch or double-tap to zoom out again.

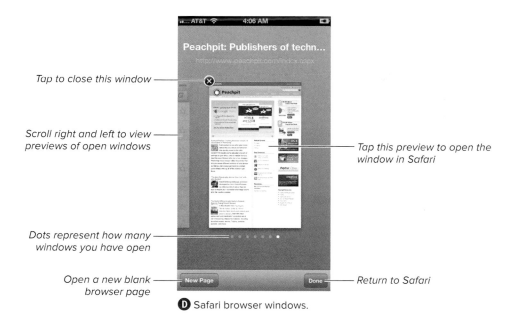

Tap to close this window

Scroll right and left to view previews of open windows

Tap this preview to open the window in Safari

Dots represent how many windows you have open

Open a new blank browser page

Return to Safari

D Safari browser windows.

To save bookmarks:

1. When you're on a page you wish to bookmark, tap the actions button in the middle of bottom the menu and tap Bookmark **B**.

2. Enter a title for the bookmark on the Add Bookmark **E** screen.

3. Tap Bookmarks Bar and choose a folder for this new bookmark.

4. Tap Save to save your bookmark.

To view or edit bookmarks:

- Tap the Bookmarks button. Tap an item to open it in Safari. Edit this list by tapping the Edit button and tapping the red delete icon next to an item in the list.

   Tapping Edit also displays the New Folder button, which lets you create a new folder for your bookmarks.

The reading list

The reading list stores web pages for you to read on any iCloud-enabled devices on- or off-line. You can do the following:

- **Add the current web page:** Tap the Actions button, and then tap the Add to Reading List icon **B**. With iPhone 4 or later, the web page is saved as well as the link, so you can read it even when you can't connect to the Internet.

- **View your reading list:** Tap the bookmark button, and then tap Reading List. Unread displays items you've not yet visited on this list. All displays both read and unread items. Tap an item to read it.

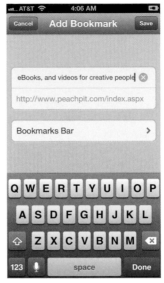

E Add Bookmark.

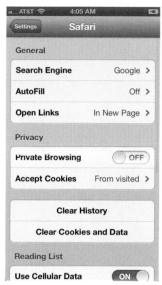

F Safari Settings.

- **Delete an item from the reading list:** Swipe a listing in the reading list. The Delete button appears. Tap it to remove the item.

TIP iCloud can keep your bookmarks and reading list up to date on other iCloud-enabled devices. To activate it, go to Settings > iCloud and slide the Safari control to On.

Changing Safari settings

Choose Settings > Safari to open Safari settings **F**, which include the following:

- **Search Engine:** By default, the iPhone uses Google search. You can switch to Yahoo! or Bing.

- **AutoFill:** Fills out some web-form fields for you using your contact information.

- **Open Links:** Open links in a new page or in the background.

- **Privacy:** These four options, Private Browsing, Accept Cookies, Clear History, and Clear Cookies and Data, control what information about your browsing your iPhone tracks or keeps.

  Turn on Private Browsing if you don't want your iPhone to remember what sites you visited. For more privacy, tap Clear History, and Clear Cookies and Data.

- **Use Cellular Data:** When On, the content of web pages in your reading list will be downloaded with your cellular network. This can run up your data usage.

- **Fraud Warning:** Gives you a heads-up if a site you visit may not be what it presents itself as being.

Using Newsstand

 Newsstand, an icon on your Home screen, is less an app and more a folder that organizes a special kind of content app: a newspaper and magazine subscription.

To subscribe to Newsstand apps:

1. The first time you open Newsstand, you'll see a link to the App Store .

2. Tap this link to see the App Store screen listing magazines and newspapers you can subscribe to.

3. Subscribe to periodicals in the App Store the same way you'd buy an app (see Chapter 8, "Getting and Using New Apps").

4. When you purchase a subscription, new issues will automatically appear in your Newsstand shelf each month.

A Newsstand.

TIP When new issues arrive, you'll see a red badge on the Newsstand app icon in the Home screen with a number indicating the number of new issues.

TIP Buying a new subscription means that the account you set up with your Apple ID will be charged (to set up an account, see Chapter 8).

Managing Newsstand apps

Ways to manage Newsstand apps include the following:

- Read a Newsstand app by tapping the icon in the Newsstand folder.

- Close a Newsstand app by tapping the Home button. This takes you back to main Newsstand screen. Tap again to return the Home screen.

- Delete a Newsstand app by tapping on and holding an icon in Newsstand. When the icons begin to wiggle, tap the x icon in the corner of the app you wish to delete.

- Each Newsstand app has options built into its interface, and they're all different. Experiment with each app to figure out what options you have.

To turn off the automatic downloading of new issues:

- Go to Settings > Newsstand and switch Automatic Content Download to Off.

Reading with iBooks

 Although iBooks doesn't come preinstalled on your iPhone, it's an Apple app that's free and worth installing. This app lets you shop for books and read them on your iPhone or other Apple device. It's also iCloud enabled, so anything you buy on one device you can read on the other, with all the devices keeping track of the current page you're on.

To get the iBooks app:

1. Open the App Store app.

2. Tap Search from the bottom menu bar.

3. Search for iBooks. Tap on the first result that says iBooks.

4. On the iBooks app result screen **A**, tap the Open button. iBooks will install.

TIP The first time you open iBooks, you'll be asked if you want to sync your bookmarks, notes, and collections between devices. If you have more than one Apple device that is iCloud connected, select Sync. (If you're not asked, you can sync bookmarks and collection under Settings > iBooks.)

Using the iBookstore

iBooks is a book reader, but it also contains the iBookstore that lets you shop for books right on your iPhone. When you've associated credit card information with your Apple ID, you can easily purchase books directly from the iBookstore with a single click.

A Search result for iBooks in the App Store.

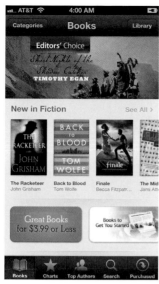

B iBookstore.

C Book information.

Open iBooks and tap the Store button to open it. The iBookstore **B** has five main sections accessible by tapping the icons in the toolbar at the bottom of the app. These are, from left to right, Books, Charts, Top Authors, Search, and Purchased.

TIP The Categories button on the top of the Books, Charts, and Top Authors screens allows you to filter the books to just one category. Or you can tap All Categories to see all app categories.

- **Books:** The Books screen **B** has several sections that may vary depending on what books Apple is trying to promote. Under each section is a set of recommended books. Each of these books displays the title and author. Swipe to the left to see more books.

  Each section has a See All link that you can tap to view all the recommended books, and more recommendations, in a list.

  Scroll down to the bottom of the app to see the Redeem and Apple ID buttons. If you have a gift card, tap to enter and redeem it. The Apple ID button should display your Apple ID. If it doesn't, tap it and enter the requested information.

  When you tap on a book icon, you see an information screen where you can view the book's rating, read more about the book, read reviews, and purchase the book **C**.

continues on next page

- **Charts:** The Charts **D** screen displays the most popular books and a tab for the New York Times bestsellers. The two sections are Paid Books and Free Books. Swipe to the left to see more books, or tap See All to see a list view.

- **Top Authors:** Top Authors **E** gives you a list of popular authors. Tap an author to see a list of that author's books available in the iBookstore. Use the small letters running down the side of the screen to jump through the list based on last name.

- **Search:** Search **F** is exactly that: a search box. Tap to type in a title or author for a book. Start typing, and as you type, a list of suggestions appears. Tap any of the results to see books fitting your search.

  Clear the search box by tapping the x icon to the right.

- **Purchased:** This screen gives you a list of all iBookstore books you've ever purchased. If you bought an iBook on another device and have iCloud enabled, you can download that book to your iPhone.

D Charts.

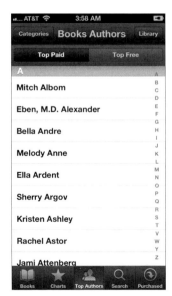

E Top Authors.

F Search the iBookstore.

G iBookstore.

To shop for books with iBooks:

1. Open the iBooks app.

2. Tap the Store button on the upper right. The iBookstore opens **G**.

3. Browse by using the menu bar options at the bottom, tap the Categories button to narrow down the results, or tap Search to look for a specific word in a title or author.

4. To view more information about a book, tap its icon. To purchase, tap the button with a price on it (or tap Free).

5. The book will automatically be loaded into your iBooks app.

6. Tap Library to return to your iBooks bookshelf.

TIP You can find lots of free books in the iBooks store. Tap Charts and look for the Free Books section. Tap See All to view a list.

TIP In addition to buying books with the iBookstore, you can read ePub and PDF documents. To get them on your iPhone, connect your iPhone to iTunes on your computer and drag these types of documents onto your iPhone icon.

Organizing your iBooks

When you buy an iBook, it's automatically delivered to your bookshelf **H**. The default view of your books is a screen containing a bookshelf graphic. As you get more books, the bookshelf view can become cluttered. Changing it to List view can help, as can using iBooks' collections feature to organize your books into groups.

TIP To get to your bookshelf from the iBookstore or while reading a book, tap the Library button.

View collections

Tap Edit and select a book to delete it

Search title and author

Visit iBookstore

Switch to list view

H Bookshelf view.

① Search box, revealed when you swipe downward from the top of the screen.

To change the bookshelf view to List view:

1. Swipe downward to reveal a search box and view options **①**.

2. Tap the list view button **①** to switch views.

   List view allows you to sort your books by titles, authors, and categories.

View collections

Tap Edit and select a book to delete it

Search title and author

Visit iBookstore

Switch to bookshelf view

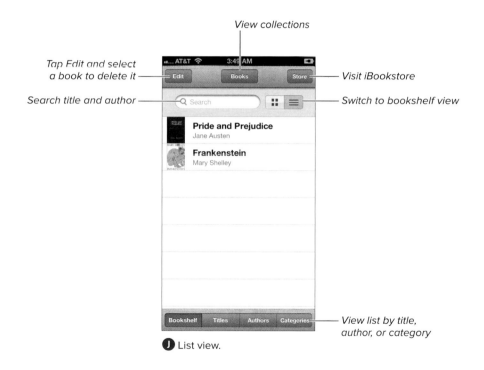

View list by title, author, or category

① List view.

View your bookshelf and tap the Collections button to open your collections list . You can use collections to do the following:

- Assign a book to a collection by tapping Edit on the bookshelf screen, tapping the book, and tapping Move. The Collections screen opens. Tap the collection you want this book to be in.

- Create a collection by tapping New on the Collections screen and typing in a new name. Tap Done.

- Tap Edit in the Collections screen to delete a collection by tapping the red delete icon, or change the order of the collections by dragging the handles on the right up and down.

TIP When you delete a collection, you'll be asked if you want to delete the collection's contents as well. If you do delete a book accidentally this way, you can always go back to the Purchased page of the iBookstore and get it back for free.

To delete a book from your bookshelf:

1. View your bookshelf and tap Edit.

2. Select the book you wish to remove. Tap Delete.

3. Tap Delete on the confirmation.

TIP Deleting a book this way only removes it from your bookshelf (and your iPhone), but you can always go back to the Purchased page of the iBookstore and get it back for free.

Add a new collection ——— New
Return to bookshelf
Currently selected collection
Edit, delete, or reorder collections

K Collections.

Reading an iBook

Once you've bought a book with the iBookstore, you can begin reading it.

To read a book with iBooks:

1. Open your iBooks app. If you're in the iBooks store, tap the Library button in the upper right of the screen.

2. Tap on a book on your shelf. The iBook opens ❶.

3. To turn pages, swipe right to left on the screen (or left to right to back up a page). Or tap the right side of the screen to turn the page or the left to go back.

TIP You might find it easier to read turning your iPhone horizontally (landscape mode).

Change brightness, font size, font, and theme

View table of contents, bookmarks, and notes

Search book text

Return to bookshelf

Add a bookmark

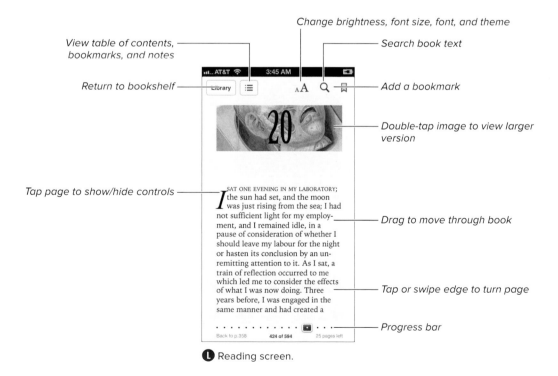

Double-tap image to view larger version

Tap page to show/hide controls

Drag to move through book

Tap or swipe edge to turn page

Progress bar

❶ Reading screen.

Your options while reading in iBooks include the following:

- **Change the type and layout:** Tap the type icon to change the screen brightness, text size, font, and theme.

- **Jump to a page:** To jump to a page, drag the slider on the page navigator. To jump by chapter, swipe left or right with three fingers at the right or left edge of the screen.

- **Bookmark a page:** Tap to bookmark a page that you want to return to. To see all your bookmarks, tap the Contents button **H** and tap Bookmarks.

- **Highlight text:** Touch and hold and then drag. Change highlight color, remove highlighting, or add a note.

- **Search:** Tap the Search icon and type in a word or phrase to search the current book.

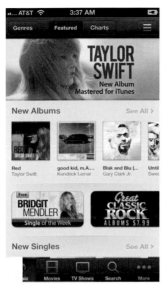

A Featured screen.

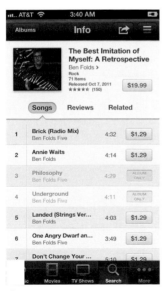

B Information screen for an album.

Shopping on iTunes

The iTunes Store app sells the same media content you see when you use the iTunes software on your computer. It's just handier. You can buy (or in some cases rent) media, including music, movies, and audiobooks.

As with the iBookstore and the App store, when you've associated credit card information with your Apple ID, you can make purchases.

Open the iTunes Store app **A** and you'll see a bottom menu bar with Music, Movies, TV Shows, Search, and More. Tap More and Audiobooks, Tones, Genius, Purchased, and Downloads appear.

Here's how the iTunes Store is organized:

- **Music, Movies, TV Shows, Audiobooks, and Tones:** All these screens have a similar structure. They have a Genre or Category button, a Featured tab, and a Charts tab.

- **Featured screen A:** This screen for each media type displays several sections. Two of these are generally devoted to new and popular offerings. Tap the See All link to view all the recommended books, and more recommendations, in a list.

When you tap an icon for an album, movie, TV show, and so forth, you see an information screen where you can view the item's rating, read more about it, read reviews, and purchase (or in the case of movies, rent) the item **B**.

TIP Depending on the type of media, the information screen might give you the chance to listen to or view a sample of the media.

continues on next page

- **Charts screen C**: This screen displays the most popular items of each type.

- **Genres or Categories screen D**: Tap a listing in this screen to limit the view of the items you see. For example, if you tap Genres on the Music screen, you could tap Blues to limit what you see on the main Music screen to Blues music only.

- **Redeem and Apple ID buttons:** Scroll down to the bottom of the Featured screen to find the Redeem and Apple ID buttons. If you have a gift card, tap to enter and redeem it. The Apple ID button should display your Apple ID. If it doesn't, tap it and enter the requested information.

C Charts screen.

D Select a genre (or category) to limit your recommendations on the Featured and Charts screens.

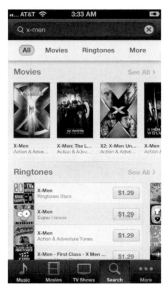

E Search screen with search results.

F Genius recommendations.

- **Search:** The top of this screen displays a search box **E**. Tap to start typing, and as you type, a list of suggestions appears. Tap a result to see any iTunes media fitting your search. Swipe to the left to see more.

- **Genius F:** Turn on Genius to get recommendations based on your previous iTunes purchases. When you switch Genius on, you have to enter your Apple ID password and agree to the terms of service.

  Tap the See All link and then swipe an entry to reveal a thumbs up/down. Tap to rate the media to fine-tune what Genius chooses.

- **Downloads:** When you purchase something big, like a movie, use this screen to watch the progress of the download.

Playing Music

You've made your purchase of an album (or an audiobook) using the iTunes Store app. Or maybe you've used iTunes on your computer, copied in an album, and then dragged the music to your connected iPhone.

You've got music on your iPhone and you'd like to listen to it.

Use the Music app.

To play music or other audio:

1. Tap the Music app in the dock. The Music app opens **A**.

2. Tap the Artists, Songs, or Albums buttons at the bottom of the screen to locate the item you wish to play.

A Music app.

Music Multitasks

One of the nice things about playing music on your iPhone is that it will keep playing while you use other apps or when the screen is locked.

You can access music controls in the lock screen by double-clicking the Home button.

When you're using another app, double-click the Home button and then swipe to the right on the dock to see the music controls.

3. Tap the item you want to play. This opens the Now Playing screen. Use the controls on the screen to fast-forward, pause, rewind, and more **B**.

TIP You can see all the tracks on the current album on the Now Playing screen by tapping on the List button in the top-right corner.

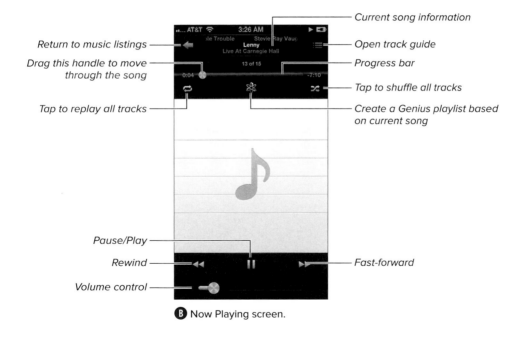

Current song information

Return to music listings

Open track guide

Drag this handle to move through the song

Progress bar

Tap to shuffle all tracks

Tap to replay all tracks

Create a Genius playlist based on current song

Pause/Play

Rewind — Fast-forward

Volume control

B Now Playing screen.

Playing Videos

 Videos is your go-to app when you rent or buy a movie or a TV show or just want to watch video you've captured with your iPhone's camera (see Chapter 12, "Creating").

To play videos:

1. Tap the Videos app in the dock. The Videos app opens **A**.

2. Tap the item you want to play. (If you have multiple devices with iCloud, you may want to tap the Shared icon and choose your library.)

3. Use the controls on the screen to fast-forward, pause, rewind, and more **B**.

TIP You can see all the chapters in a video by tapping the List button to the left of the controls.

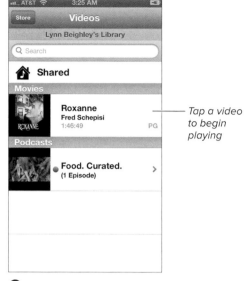

Tap a video to begin playing

A Videos app.

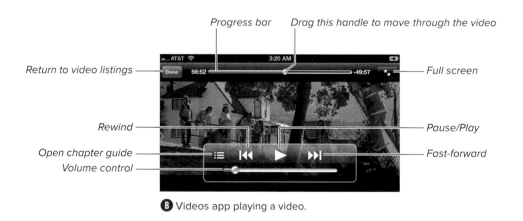

B Videos app playing a video.

Playing with Game Center

Your iPhone can help make you incredibly productive. Calendar, Reminders, Contacts, Siri, Mail, and Notes save you lots of time. They might save you too much time. Perhaps you now have a bit of free time, and you're not sure what to do with it. Or maybe you're just ready to have a little fun.

Lucky for you, there's Game Center. Game Center is an app that manages your collection of iOS games, keeping track of them and giving you an easy way to boast about your prowess to others. But it's much more than that. Use Game Center to connect with friends, and see what games they're playing and how well they are doing. Let's play.

The Game Center App

Game Center is an app that tracks your game play and lets you connect with friends to track theirs, and if you want, challenge them.

To start using Game Center:

1. Tap the Game Center icon. Game Center opens **A**.

   The first time you start it up, you may be prompted to enter an Apple ID and password. You'll need an Apple ID so that Game Center can keep track of your accomplishments in Game Center-enabled games and also to help you connect with friends.

2. To get started, enter your Apple ID and password and tap Sign In. Or create an Apple ID by tapping Create Apple ID. There's nothing else you can do with Game Center until you're signed in.

To set up your Game Center account:

1. After you sign in the first time, a Terms & Conditions screen appears. Scroll to the bottom and tap Agree. Tap Agree again on the confirmation message.

2. After you accept, a new form opens. You need to select a nickname (above and to the right).

3. Decide if you want to allow all Game Center players to be able to see your profile. If you only want your friends to be able to see it, set Public Profile to Off.

Enter your Apple ID and password and tap Sign In

If you don't have an Apple ID, tap to get one

A Game Center when you aren't logged in with an Apple ID.

4. Tap Done.

Your user profile has been created **B**. The one shown has a photo and a status message set. You can edit these and a few more items:

- Much like a Facebook status message, Game Center lets you set a status. Enter one by tapping and typing the word Status just above the Add Photo banner.

- Add (or change) your photo by tapping the Add (or Change) Photo banner. You can take a new snapshot of yourself with the camera or use an existing one.

- If you want to change your Account settings, tap the Account banner with your email address. Choose View Account and then you'll be taken back to the screen where you selected your nickname.

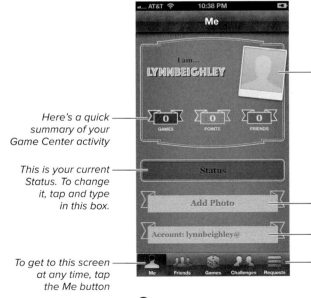

Tap to add a photo to your Game Center account. You can use an existing photo on your iPhone or take a new one.

Here's a quick summary of your Game Center activity

This is your current Status. To change it, tap and type in this box.

Tap the Add Photo banner to change your profile image. Or you can simply tap your current image to open the Change Photo dialog box.

Your email address will appear here. Tap this banner to edit your account settings.

To get to this screen at any time, tap the Me button

Now that you've set up your account and signed in, you can navigate Game Center with these buttons

B The profile displays your username, your image, a summary of how many Game Center games you play, your total points, and how many friends you have. The screen contains two banner links: Change Photo, which lets you modify your profile image, and Account:<youremail>, which allows you to change your account settings.

Connect with Friends

The point of Game Center is to see and share game scores and achievements with your friends. Adding friends is easy. Open the Friends screen by tapping the Friends button at the bottom of Game Center.

To add a friend:

1. Tap the Friends button to open the Friends screen **Ⓐ**.

After you tap this plus sign or Add Friends, the Friend Request form opens. Enter your friend's email address or Game Center username.

Tap to sort your list of friends three different ways: alphabetically, how recently they've used Game Center, or how many points they have

Ⓐ Friends screen, containing a list of all your friends.

2. Tap the plus sign in the upper left of the screen. A Friend Request opens **B**.

3. Type in your friend's email address or Game Center nickname. Customize the message if you wish.

4. Tap Send. Your friend will be notified and will have to accept the request before he shows up as your friend in Game Center.

TIP Other players can send you Friend requests. You'll get emails letting you know. It's also easy to find them in Game Center at any given moment so you can accept or ignore them.

To accept or ignore Friend requests:

1. Tap the Requests button to open the Requests screen.

2. Any pending requests will show up here. Tap on one to open it.

3. Choose Accept or Ignore. If you accept, your new friend appears in the list of your friends in the Friends screen.

TIP Should you wish to remove a friend, tap the friend's name in the friend list to open his information page and tap the Unfriend banner on the bottom of his page.

You can type here to customize the message your friend will receive

Tap Send and your friend will get a request in his email

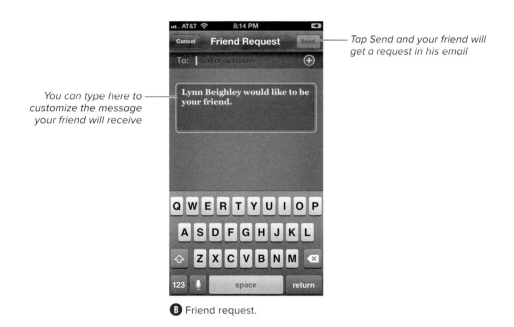

B Friend request.

Find and Buy Games

You've got your account and your friends. Now you're ready to play. There are a couple of ways to find Game Center-enabled games to play.

To find Game Center games:

- Tap the Games button at the bottom of the Game Center to see recommendations and top games. Or tap the Find Game Center Games banner at the bottom of this page, which opens the App Store (see Chapter 8, "Getting and Using New Apps").

  or

- Tap the Friends button and select one of your friends. Tap the word Games to see what she plays and how well she's doing. Tap on one of the games to see more details about it.

TIP You can view or purchase the game your friend is playing by tapping the Price button. This takes you to the App store, where you can buy the game.

Challenge a Friend

When you and your friend play the same games, you can challenge him to reach a game achievement.

To challenge a friend:

1. Tap the Friends button.

2. Locate and tap on a friend. This opens a profile for this friend .

3. If it's not selected, tap Games to see what games you and your friend have in common.

4. Tap a game you both play.

continues on next page

This is your currently selected friend's stats. Tap on each of these to see more specific information about what games he plays, where he's earned points, and who his friends are.

Ⓐ Profile of a friend.

5. Tap the Achievements link.

6. Choose from the achievements your friend hasn't reached. Tap one, and then tap Send Challenge .

7. The Send Challenge screen opens. Send as is or add a personal message. Tap Send.

   Your friend will get the message, and if he accepts, his name will appear in the Challenge screen.

🅑 List of achievements possible for this game.

Keeping
Track

As you might guess, Calendar is a calendar app. It keeps track of your events and sends notifications, among other things, to remind you. Calendar is a great tool for keeping track of family activities or for coordinating corporate events. You can create separate calendars for separate parts of your life.

When you need something quick and easy and less robust, use Reminders. This feature keeps a checklist of tasks you need to accomplish, stored on a calendar in the app. As with Calendar, Reminders can send you notifications and emails.

Better still, iCloud, Apple's automatic and free storage and syncing solution, keeps your Calendar and Reminders synced to all of your computers and mobile devices.

In This Chapter

Navigating the Calendar

The Calendar app lets you switch between views of your days and events with just a tap. View a month at a time **A**, a day **B**, a week (day view in landscape mode) **C**, or a list of upcoming events **D**; go back in time or forward into the future. Set recurring Events to happen every first Friday or every three months. Create Reminders that are attached to certain calendars. Turn calendars on or off so you can view just individual ones, or view several at a time to see how your events overlap.

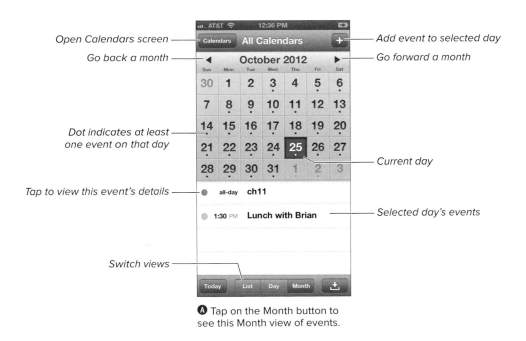

Open Calendars screen

Go back a month

Dot indicates at least one event on that day

Tap to view this event's details

Switch views

Add event to selected day

Go forward a month

Current day

Selected day's events

A Tap on the Month button to see this Month view of events.

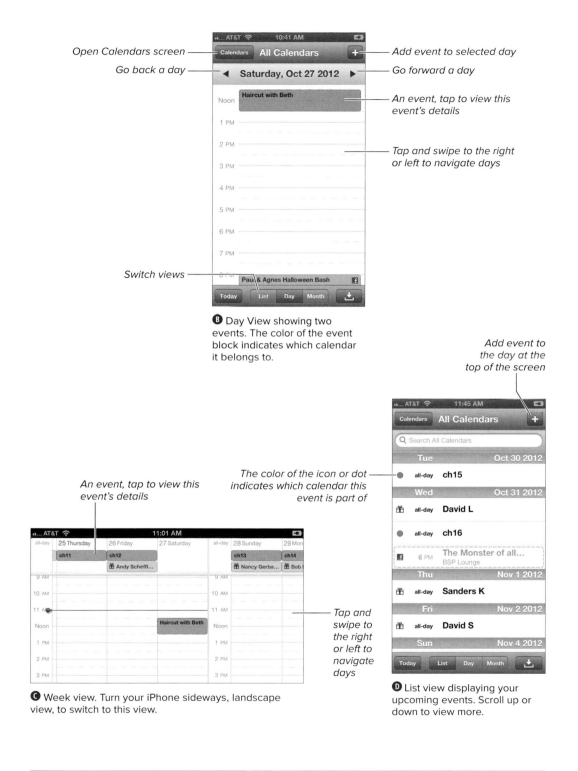

Open Calendars screen —— Calendars **All Calendars** +

Add event to selected day

Go back a day —— ◀ **Saturday, Oct 27 2012** ▶

Go forward a day

Noon Haircut with Beth

An event, tap to view this event's details

Tap and swipe to the right or left to navigate days

Switch views ——

Pau. & Agnes Halloween Bash

Today   List   Day   Month

B Day View showing two events. The color of the event block indicates which calendar it belongs to.

Add event to the day at the top of the screen

Calendars **All Calendars** +

Q Search All Calendars

Tue   Oct 30 2012
● all-day **ch15**
Wed   Oct 31 2012
⊞ all-day **David L**
● all-day **ch16**
      6 PM The Monster of all...
            BSP Lounge
Thu   Nov 1 2012
⊞ all-day **Sanders K**
Fri   Nov 2 2012
⊞ all-day **David S**
Sun   Nov 4 2012

Today   List   Day   Month

The color of the icon or dot indicates which calendar this event is part of

An event, tap to view this event's details

all-day | 25 Thursday | 26 Friday | 27 Saturday | all-day | 28 Sunday | 29 Mon
| ch11 | ch12 | | | ch13 | ch14
| | ⊞ Andy Scheffl... | | | ⊞ Nancy Gerba... | ⊞ Bob

Haircut with Beth

Tap and swipe to the right or left to navigate days

C Week view. Turn your iPhone sideways, landscape view, to switch to this view.

D List view displaying your upcoming events. Scroll up or down to view more.

Linking External Calendars

You're not limited to creating calendars on your iPhone. You can also link in data from Microsoft Exchange, Google, or Yahoo! calendars.

You can set up those calendars by adding new accounts to your iPhone.

To link third-party calendars to your iPhone calendar:

1. Go to Settings > Mail, Contacts, Calendars.

2. Tap Add Account. Tap on the type of calendar you want to add **Ⓐ**.

3. Enter the information. Generally this is your name, email, password, and, optionally, a description of the account **Ⓑ**. Tap Next.

Ⓐ Add Account screen.

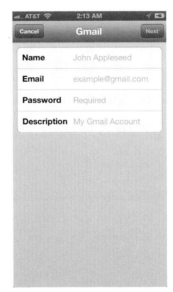

Ⓑ Fill in account info for the account with the calendar you want to link to.

C Make sure Calendars is set to On in the account settings.

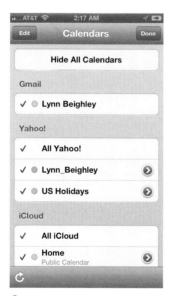

D Calendars view from the Calendar app. Tap to check/uncheck calendars. Unchecking won't delete them; it just hides the unchecked calendars' events from the calendar.

4. Make sure the Calendars slider is set to On **C**. Tap Save. Your calendar from the account you just added will now appear in your iPhone Calendar app.

5. Close Settings and tap Calendar to open it.

6. Tap the Calendars button on the upper left to see the list of calendars. The new one you just added should appear **D**.

TIP If the account you just linked allows you to create more than one calendar, you'll see that reflected on the Calendars page.

TIP You can add your Facebook events to your calendar. Go to Settings > Facebook, sign in to your Facebook account, and slide the Calendar control to On.

Creating Calendars

You can have many different calendars—one for each of your kids, one for work, one for your partner, one for home life, one for the charities you volunteer for, and so forth. Choose to see all the calendars and events at once and you'll have a visual display of just how busy your life is.

To create a new calendar:

1. Open the Calendar app and tap the Calendars button on the upper left.

2. Tap the Edit button. This opens the Edit Calendars screen **Ⓐ**.

   Scroll down to the On My iPhone section and tap Add Calendar.

   or

   If you have iCloud enabled, scroll down the iCloud section and tap Add Calendar.

3. Type in a name for your new calendar and select a color for it **Ⓑ**. Tap Done.

4. Your new calendar appears in the iCloud list.

Ⓐ Edit Calendars screen.

Ⓑ Add Calendar screen.

To delete a calendar:

1. Open the Calendar app and tap the Calendars button on the upper left.

2. Tap the Edit button. This opens the Edit Calendars screen Ⓐ. Tap the calendar you wish to delete.

3. Scroll to the bottom of the page and tap Delete Calendar. A confirmation pane appears. Tap Delete Calendar again.

To hide calendars without deleting:

1. Open the Calendar app and tap the Calendars button on the upper left.

2. Tap to uncheck any calendars you do not want to appear or tap Hide All Calendars.

TIP Hiding a calendar will also keep you from getting reminders from it.

Creating Events

An event is something that happens on a particular day, maybe at a specific time.

To create an event:

1. In List, Month, or Day view, tap the + button in the upper-right corner. The Add Event screen opens 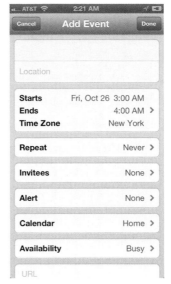.

2. Tap and enter a title and a location for your event.

3. Tap the Starts and Ends section. This opens the Start & End screen **B**.

4. Select Starts. Tap and slide the wheels at the bottom of the screen to select the date and time. Repeat with the Ends time. Or, if the event doesn't have a time or is an all-day event, slide All-day to On.

5. If the Time Zone is incorrect, tap it, and enter the name of a city that is in the correct time zone. Tap Done.

TIP Calendar arranges multiple events on one day according to the times you enter.

A Add Event screen.

B Start & End screen.

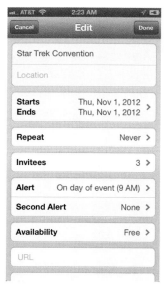

C Event Details screen.

Additional Event Options

Title, location, and start and end time are all you really have to enter to create an event. But there are a number of additional settings worth using. These are:

- **Repeat:** If you want this event to repeat—for example, it's a weekly meeting—use this to choose from Every Day, Every Week, Every 2 Weeks, Every Month, or Every Year.

- **Invitees:** You can invite other people to your event. See "Managing Event Invitations" later in this chapter for more information.

- **Alert:** Set an event alert if you want your iPhone to notify you before the event. Your options range from *At the time of the event* or *5 minutes before* to *2 days before*.

- **Calendar:** Pick which of your calendars you want this event to be associated with. This is what dictates what color the event will be on your calendar.

- **Availability:** If you share your calendar, this setting tells other people whether you are busy or free during the event.

To edit or delete an event:

1. Open Calendar. Locate the event and tap on it.

2. This opens the Event Details screen **C**. Tap the Edit button.

3. From this screen, you can change any of the event settings. When finished, tap Done.

4. To delete this event, scroll to the bottom of the screen and tap Delete Event. Confirm by tapping Delete Event again and your event has been deleted.

Managing Event Invitations

From the Calendar app you can send someone an invitation to a Calendar Event. The invitee can send a response that shows up in that Event Details panel.

To send a Calendar Event invitation:

1. Create a new event, or tap an existing event in Calendar.

2. In the Event Details screen, tap Edit.

TIP Oddly enough, you can edit events that already happened. If you do, though, you won't see the Invitees option. That makes sense—you wouldn't want to invite someone to something that already happened.

3. Tap Invitees. This opens the Add Invitees email screen **A**.

4. Start typing in the To field. Your iPhone will guess who you want to send this to based on your Contacts. You can type multiple addresses in the To field.

   If the person you want to send it to isn't in your Contacts, go ahead and type his full email address.

5. You can type multiple addresses. When you're done, tap Done. Your invitees will receive an email message with the event information.

Tap to open Contacts list

A Add Invitees email screen.

B Event notification email.

To respond to an email event notification:

1. When you receive an email that contains a Calendar Event attachment **B**, tap the attachment icon at the bottom of the message to automatically put the Event in Calendar.

2 Go to Calendar and double-click the Event that was added automatically. In the Event Info panel that opens, respond with an option: Accept, Maybe, or Decline.

3. The organizer of the Event receives an email with a Calendar attachment. When he clicks the attachment, the response is added to the Event in *his* Calendar. He can view the Event in Calendar to open the Event Info panel and see the responses of invitees.

Syncing Calendar Events with iCloud

Here's the quick scoop on getting your Calendar synced with iCloud so it works with your other Apple devices. This assumes you already have an iCloud account set up. (If you don't, take a look at Chapter 5, "Managing Your Settings.")

To sync Calendar with iCloud:

1. Go to Settings > iCloud.

2. If you need to, enter your Apple ID and password and tap Sign In. Your iPhone logs you in and the iCloud Settings page appears **A**.

3. On the iCloud Settings page, make sure that Calendars is set to On.

Your Calendar data will now sync with Calendar apps on every other iCloud-enabled device you use.

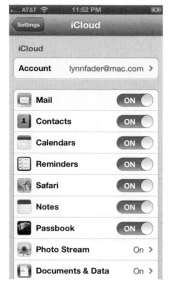

A iCloud settings with Calendars set to On.

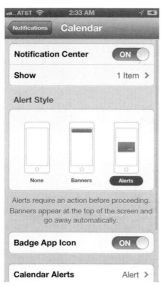

A Notifications settings for the Calendar app.

Getting Event Notifications

You can, and do by default, get notifications from your Calendar Events as soon as the time and date of the event arrives. You can control whether or not you receive Calendar notifications, what form they take, and how many you receive. You can learn more about notifications in Chapter 6, "Handling Notifications."

To manage Calendar notifications:

1. Go to Settings > Notifications > Calendar **A**.

2. Make sure Notification Center is set to On.

3. Choose how many calendar events you want to appear in Notification Center, the screen that appears when you swipe downward from the status bar.

4. You can also change the style of notification and whether your Calendar icon will display a red badge with the number of new event notifications you've received in it.

Publishing Your Calendar

You can publish your calendar to iCloud if you choose, and anyone in the world on any computer connected to the Internet can view it.

To publish your calendar:

1. Open the Calendar app and tap the Calendars button. Tap the blue icon to the right of the calendar you want to publish.
2. Swipe down to the bottom of the Edit Calendar screen and switch Public Calendar to On (A).
3. Tap Share Link to email or message the link to someone.
4. A new mail form or message form appears telling you the web address where the calendar can be viewed. Address the mail or message and tap Send.

   Or tap Copy to save the link to your public site to your clipboard.

To unpublish your calendar:

- Follow the previous steps to choose a calendar; then from the Calendar menu (A) slide Public Calendar to Off.

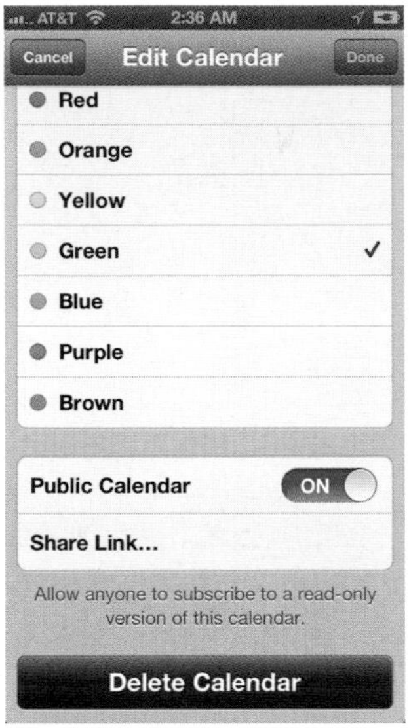

(A) Edit Calendar screen.

A List view.

Creating Reminders

When you need to make a quick list of tasks to get done, Calendar might be overkill. The Reminders app lets you quickly create lists of things to get done, or reminders. As with Calendar, you can configure it to send you Notifications and sync with iCloud.

To navigate Reminders:

- Reminders are organized in lists **A**. Tapping a list brings up its reminders **B**. You can create reminders that are due by a certain date or that notify you when you arrive at a specific destination **C**.

B Reminders view.

C Details screen for a reminder.

To create a list:

1. Open Reminders. If the List view **A** is not open, tap the List button (upper left, with three small lines on it).

2. Tap Create New List and type the name of your list.

   Once you have a list, you can add reminders to it.

TIP If you mess up or if you want to change the name of a list, tap the Edit button on the List view, tap on the list name you want to change, and retype the name of your list.

To create a reminder:

1. If the List view **A** is not open, tap the List button on the top left.

2. Tap the list where you want to add a reminder.

3. In the Reminders view **B**, tap in a blank space and type in your reminder. Or tap the plus sign.

4. Tap on the gray > icon to the right of the reminder to open its Details screen **C**. Tap Show More.

   Prioritize your item, add a note, give it a due date, make it notify you when you reach a destination (with location services enabled), and more. Tap Done.

5. When the item has been completed, tap in the completed check-box.

TIP When you check off a Reminder, it disappears from the current list and shows up in the Completed list **D**. You can restore it by tapping on the Completed list in List view and unchecking it.

D Completed reminders list.

E Location Services with both Location Services and Reminders set to On.

F Details for a reminder with Remind Me At a Location turned on.

To move a reminder from one list to another:

1. Tap on the gray > icon next to the reminder you want to move to open its Details **C**.

2. Tap Show More and tap List.

3. Choose the list you want the reminder in.

To create a location-based reminder:

1. Location Services needs to be turned on. Go to Settings > Privacy > Location Services. Switch both Location Services and Reminders to On **E**.

2. Open Reminders and tap on the gray > icon next to the reminder you want to make location-based **C**.

3. Slide the Remind Me At a Location control to On. An address appears under the control **F**.

4. **Tap the gray** > icon next to the address to enter a new address. Enter the address and tap Details when you're done.

5. Choose either When I Leave or When I Arrive. Tap Done.

To sync Reminders with iCloud:

1. Go to Settings > iCloud.

2. If you need to, enter your Apple ID and password and tap Sign In. Your iPhone logs you in and the iCloud settings page appears.

3. On the iCloud settings page, make sure that Reminders is set to On.

Your Reminders data will now sync with Reminders apps on every other iCloud-enabled device you use.

Creating

As if calling, sending emails, web browsing, planning, and playing games with your
iPhone weren't enough, you can also take
pictures and videos, and create written
works with it. Your iPhone comes with the
Camera app (and an excellent built-in camera) for taking photos, panorama images,
and videos. Use the Photos app to organize and share your images. And when
your images inspire you, start up the Notes
app to create great written works.
Or just take notes.

In this chapter, you'll learn how to create
things with your iPhone.

In This Chapter

Using Camera Controls

 The Camera app is simple to use **Ⓐ**. From this app you can swap between taking photos or video and switch between the front, lower-quality camera to the better rear camera. You can view photos you've taken and tap the screen to focus your shots. If you pinch or spread your thumb and finger on the screen, you can zoom in or out.

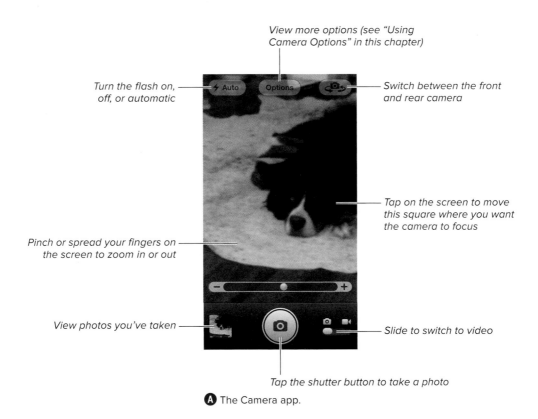

View more options (see "Using Camera Options" in this chapter)

Turn the flash on, off, or automatic

Switch between the front and rear camera

Tap on the screen to move this square where you want the camera to focus

Pinch or spread your fingers on the screen to zoom in or out

View photos you've taken

Slide to switch to video

Tap the shutter button to take a photo

Ⓐ The Camera app.

Tap and drag the camera upward to reveal the Camera app

B The Camera button in the lock screen.

To take a photo:

1. Tap the Camera app to open it.

   Or, if you're in the lock screen, tap and drag the camera icon up **B**.

2. Zoom in or out and tap on the screen to adjust the focus.

3. Tap the round shutter button.

Recording Locations in Your Photos

The Camera app asks you if it can use location information the first time you start it. This Information allows it to embed the location where the photo was taken in the photo's data. You can see this information in most photo-editing programs. It's useful if you want to keep track of where you took your photos.

For the locations of your photos to be saved, you need to switch on Location Services (Settings > Privacy > Location Services) and the Camera option under Location Services (Settings > Privacy > Location Services > Camera).

TIP You're not stuck only taking portrait type (tall, vertical) photos. You can switch to landscape (wide, horizontal) photos just by turning the camera on its side before you take your photo.

Using Camera Options

Tap the Options button to view additional settings to help you take better photos .

- Use Grid to display a grid while you're taking your photo. This won't appear on the actual photo.

- HDR (High Dynamic Range) gives you a better-quality photo by taking three photos of the same thing and combining them to give you the best results of the three-in-one photo.

- The third option is a button that lets you take a panorama shot. Panoramas are really, really long (or tall) photos composed of a series of smaller photos **B**.

A Tap the Options button on the Camera app to see these options.

B A panorama shot. Tap the Panorama option and begin moving your camera across the horizon.

C The screen you see when you are taking a panorama. The arrow will move along the line as you record the shot.

To take a panorama photo:

1. In the Camera app, tap the Options button.

2. Tap the Panorama button to open the Panorama screen **C**.

3. Tap the round shutter button to begin your photo.

4. Slowly move your camera horizontally, left to right, to take your photo.

5. An arrow begins moving along a line on the screen. When you tilt the camera up or down, the arrow moves off the line, which messes up the shot.
   Try to keep the arrow on the line.

6. When you're done, tap Done.

TIP The Panorama screen will give you helpful feedback as you take the photo. You may be told to slow down or to keep the arrow on the line.

Making Videos

The Camera app is also the app to go to when you want to create a video. Open the Camera app and slide the control on the bottom right to the movie camera icon **Ⓐ**. Instead of the shutter button, you'll see a red recording button. Tap this when you want to begin recording, and tap it again when you're done.

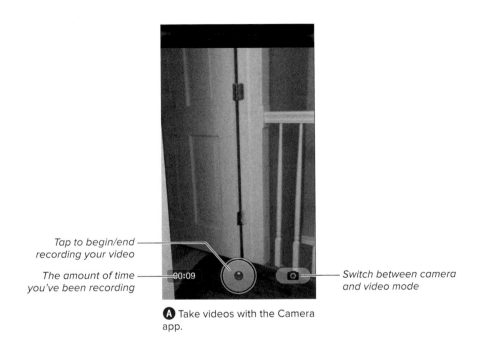

Tap to begin/end recording your video

The amount of time you've been recording

Switch between camera and video mode

Ⓐ Take videos with the Camera app.

Viewing and Sharing Photos and Videos

When you've taken photos and videos with the Camera app, you'll want to view them and maybe share them. You can see all your photos and videos in the Camera app and do all kinds of other things with them, including email, message, post to Twitter or Facebook, or use as wallpaper on your iPhone.

To view your photos and videos:

1. Open the Camera app in portrait mode.

2. Tap the thumbnail image on the bottom left. (This is a thumbnail of the last photo or video you took.)

3. You're viewing the last photo or video you took **A**. From this screen you can tap and drag to the left and right to view other images you've taken.

TIP When you're viewing images you've taken, after a second the controls will disappear. Just tap the screen to make them show again.

continues on next page

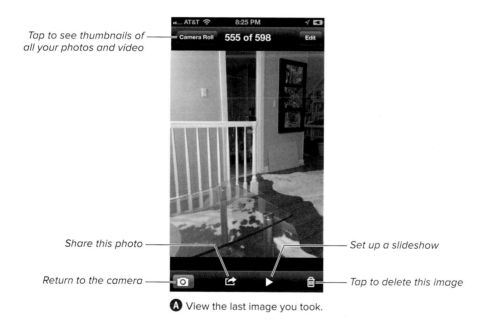

Tap to see thumbnails of all your photos and video

Share this photo

Return to the camera

Set up a slideshow

Tap to delete this image

A View the last image you took.

4. To see thumbnails of everything you've got stored, tap the Camera Roll button.

TIP If your Camera Roll contains more than 20 images, drag your finger up to scroll more images into view. To see a picture or movie full screen, tap it.

5. Tap on a thumbnail to view that image or video. You can play a video by tapping on the play button.

6. You can tap the Delete button to delete the current image or video you're viewing **B**.

7. To return to camera mode, tap the blue camera button.

To view a slideshow of your photos:

1. Open the Camera app in portrait mode.

2. Tap the thumbnail image on the bottom left. You're viewing the last photo or video you took **A**.

   To use the slideshow, you need to be viewing a photo, so either drag the screen to the right until you are viewing a photo, or tap the Camera Roll button.

3. Tap the slideshow button (it looks like a play button). This opens the Slideshow Options **C**.

4. You can modify the transition effect between slides, and add music from your stored track in the Music app.

5. Tap Start Slideshow and it begins. To turn it off, tap the screen.

To share your photos and videos:

1. Open the Camera app in portrait mode.

2. Tap the thumbnail image on the bottom left, then tap Camera Roll.

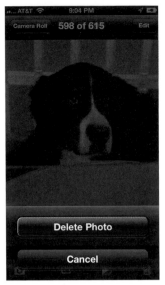

B This confirmation screen appears when you tap the Trash can button to delete an image.

C Slideshow options.

D Camera app Sharing Options.

3. Locate and tap on the photo or video you want to share. This opens the Sharing Options screen **D**.

The sharing options are as follows:

- Email a photo or video.

- Message a photo or video.

- Add this photo or video to the Photo Stream. You can send your photo to the Photo Stream if you have an iCloud account and Settings > iCloud > Photo Stream set to On. Any pictures you add to the Photo Stream are shared from the iCloud with all your iCloud-enabled devices.

- Tweet or post your photo or video to Facebook, along with a status message. Twitter or Facebook needs to be set up (Settings > Twitter > Add Account or Settings > Facebook).

- You can take a photo of a friend and use Assign to Contact to make this photo show up on a contact's listing (see Chapter 13, "Communicating").

- If you have an AirPrint printer set up (see Chapter 15, "Extending Your Phone"), you can print your photo.

- Copy the image to paste somewhere.

- Use a photo as your iPhone's wallpaper.

To transfer photos and videos to your computer:

1. Connect your iPhone to your computer.

2. Choose the Import command in the photo editor or viewer software of your choice to copy your photo and video files to the computer.

TIP On the Mac, the iPhoto program automatically detects new images on your iPhone and prompts you about uploading them.

Using the Photos App

The Photos app lets you organize, edit, and create slideshows from the photos you've taken. And the Photos app can play your videos too.

Understanding the Photos app

The Photos app has several components, some of which are optional:

- The **Albums** screen Ⓐ is home for the images stored on your camera. Use this screen to create new albums and add photos and videos to albums (see the task "To add photos and videos to albums" later in this chapter).

  Before you've added any albums, you'll see Camera Roll, which contains all your photos and videos. It also contains any images that have been sent to you by email, images from iCloud's Photo Stream, and images you've copied from Safari.

- **Photo Stream** Ⓑ appears if you have an iCloud account and Settings > iCloud > Photo Stream set to On. Any pictures added to the iCloud's Photo Stream will appear here.

- **Faces** or **Places** appears if you use iPhoto on your Mac to add information about people or events in your photos and then sync with iTunes.

> **TIP** You'll see the sharing button with the same options that the Camera app has when you drill down to an individual photo or video in the Photos app. Read more about these options in the "To share your photos and videos" task earlier in this chapter.

Ⓐ Photos app Album screen. The Camera Roll is permanent and contains all of your photos, images, and videos saved on this iPhone

Ⓑ Your Photo Stream and custom photo streams you've added.

C When you tap Add, you'll see your current albums. Tap and navigate to the images or videos you want to add to this album.

D Tap on images to add them to an album and tap Done when you're finished.

To add an album:

- Open the Photos app and tap the Albums button on the bottom menu bar **A**. Tap the + button. Enter the name for your new album and tap Save.

To remove an album:

- Open the Photos app and tap the Albums button on the bottom menu bar. Tap the Edit button. Tap the red delete icon next to any album you wish to delete. This does not permanently delete images in the album; it just removes the album.

To add photos and videos to albums:

1. Open the Photos app and tap the Albums button on the bottom menu bar **A**.

2. Tap on the album to which you want to add images. Tap Edit, then tap Add **C**. You'll see your current Albums screen.

3. Tap and navigate through your Camera Roll to find images you want to add.

4. Tap the photos or videos you want to add, and tap Done **D**.

To remove photos and videos from albums:

1. Open the Photos app and tap the Albums button on the bottom menu bar **Ⓐ**.

2. Tap on the album from which you want to remove images. Tap Edit, and then tap any images you want to remove **Ⓔ**.

3. Tap Remove.

Ⓔ Tap any images or videos you want to remove.

Editing Photos and Videos

The Photos app gives you some limited editing capabilities. You can rotate, enhance, and crop images and remove red-eye. You can also trim videos.

To use the Photos' app editing options, tap Albums and find the image you wish to edit. Tap the Edit button Ⓐ.

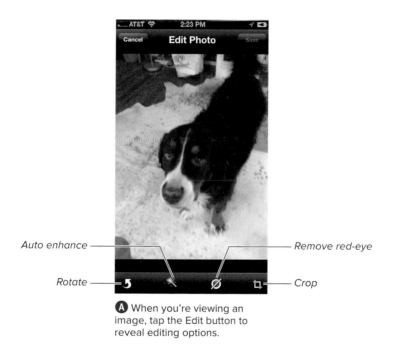

Auto enhance

Rotate

Remove red-eye

Crop

Ⓐ When you're viewing an image, tap the Edit button to reveal editing options.

Image-editing options

The options include:

- **Rotate:** Tap the Rotate button to turn the image 90 degrees counterclockwise.

- **Auto Enhance:** This will try to improve the image by adjusting contrast, brightness, and color saturation.

- **Remove Red-Eye:** Tap this option and then tap on a red eye in the image. You can use your thumb and finger to zoom in to get a better shot at tapping the red eye. The area should turn black. If Photos can't find any red, it tells you.

  When you're done, tap the Apply button in the top-right corner of the screen. Or, you can tap the eye again to undo and try again.

- **Crop:** You can crop out parts of an image you don't want with the Crop button. Tap Crop and your image shrinks so you can see all of it. Tap and drag a corner to resize the image. When you're done, tap Save or Cancel to revert to the original version.

  Crop also offers you a Constrain button that lets you choose from various crop ratios **B**.

To trim a video:

1. Open the Photos app, and locate and tap on the video you want to trim.

2. If the controls are not visible, tap the screen.

3. Tap and drag the right or left end of the frame viewer to trim frames from the beginning or end of your video **C**.

4. Tap Trim. You can choose Trim Original (which will replace the original clip) or Save as a New Clip.

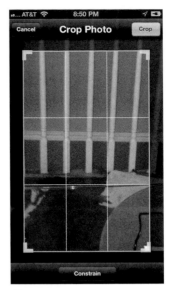

B When you choose Edit > Crop, you can drag the frame around the image.

C Drag the handles on either end of the video to trim off extra frames.

Using Notes

The Notes app is your virtual notepad. You can write quick notes to yourself and access them with iCloud on all your other devices.

To create a new note:

- Open the Notes app **A** and tap the + button in the upper right.

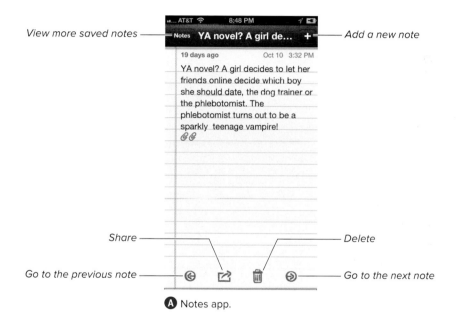

View more saved notes

Add a new note

Notes YA novel? A girl de... **+**

19 days ago   Oct 10 3:32 PM

YA novel? A girl decides to let her friends online decide which boy she should date, the dog trainer or the phlebotomist. The phlebotomist turns out to be a sparkly teenage vampire!

Share

Delete

Go to the previous note

Go to the next note

A Notes app.

Change font:

- Choose Settings > Notes . Tap to choose Noteworthy, Helvetica, or Marker Felt. This will change the font on all your notes, not just new ones.

To use spell checker:

- If a word has a red dotted line beneath it, iPhone thinks it's misspelled. Tap it once to see suggestions and tap to choose one.

  If the iPhone thinks the word is misspelled, double-tap it. A menu appears, tap the arrow on the right and then tap Suggest to see suggested spellings. Tap to choose one.

To discard a note:

- Open the note and click on the Trash can icon at the bottom. Tap Delete Note.

To share your notes via email or Messages:

- Tap the share button and choose Mail or Message.

B Notes settings where you can change the font.

Communicating

One key to easy communication is to keep your contacts list up to date. Not only can the iPhone's Contacts app be used to make phone calls, but it can be used with email, messaging, and FaceTime as well. This chapter shows you how to manage your contacts, set up email accounts, use messaging and FaceTime, and communicate with all three using your saved contacts.

In This Chapter

Managing Contacts

The Contacts app, as its name suggests, keeps your contact info for you. Contacts is integrated with Phone, Mail, and Calendar so you can easily and quickly call and send messages and invitations to your contacts. Contacts can import directories from your accounts on websites such as Yahoo! or Facebook.

Contacts can sync automatically with iCloud to keep all of your iCloud devices updated.

You can customize individual cards and/or add new fields to all of them. For instance, you can add a birthday or a nickname field. You can add a photo or image and customize the address for another country.

To add a contact:

1. Tap the Utilities folder on your Home screen to open it.
2. Tap to open the Contacts app Ⓐ.

View Groups — *Search contacts* — *Add a new contact* — *Tap a letter to navigate the alphabet* — *Tap a listing to open info for that contact*

Ⓐ The Contacts app.

B New Contact screen.

C Groups screen.

3. Tap the + sign in the top-right corner of the All Contacts page. The new, blank contact card is displayed, ready for you to add information **B**.

4. To enter data in these fields, tap the field or the green plus icon to its left.

5. To add a photo of this contact, tap the Add Photo area. This opens a sheet with the buttons Take Photo, Choose Photo, or Cancel.

   If the new contact is standing in front of you, tap Take Photo and tap the green camera icon to take a photo.

   Choose Photo lets you pick a photo already in your iPhone's saved photos.

6. Tap Done when you've entered all the contact information you wish.

TIP You can choose a unique ringtone for each contact. Tap Ringtone, and tap the ringtone you want to hear when this contact calls you.

TIP You can import accounts from third-party web accounts and email accounts. Check out the "Adding Mail Accounts" section later in this chapter for more information.

Using Groups with your Contacts

After you sync your iPhone with iTunes, you may discover that the Contacts application has a Groups button, with some of your contacts sorted into them.

The Contacts app on the iPad or on a Mac allows you to put your contacts into groups, and that's where these are coming from.

These groups appear in the Groups screen you see when you tap the Groups button in the top-left corner of the All Contacts screen **C**. Tap on a group to see the members of that group.

To edit a contact:

1. Tap the Utilities folder on your Home screen and tap Contacts. Tap a contact.

2. Tap the Edit button on the top right **D**.

3. Tap in and edit any field. To delete the information in a field entirely, tap on the red icon to the left.

4. Tap Done when you're finished.

To delete a contact:

1. Tap the Utilities folder on your Home screen and tap Contacts. Tap a contact.

2. Tap the Edit button on the top right **D**.

3. Scroll to the bottom of the screen and tap Delete Contact. Tap Delete Contact again to confirm.

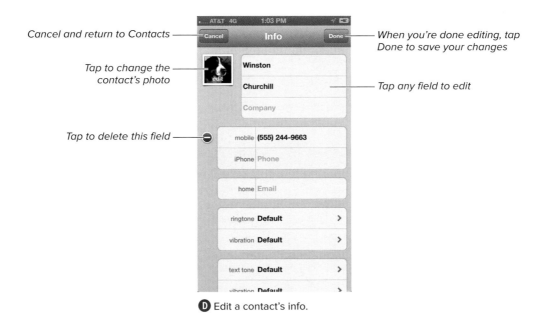

Cancel and return to Contacts

When you're done editing, tap Done to save your changes

Tap to change the contact's photo

Tap any field to edit

Tap to delete this field

D Edit a contact's info.

Using Contacts

You've added some accounts, and now you want to use the information to contact them. You have some options at your fingertips from the Contacts app.

Start by opening the Contacts app and selecting the listing for the person you want to contact. You'll see the Info screen for this person **Ⓐ**.

To call a contact:

- Tap on one of the phone number entries for this person. Your Phone app starts up and immediately dials.

To email a contact:

- Tap on the email address for this contact. Your Mail app opens with the To field filled out with the email address. Type a subject and message and tap Send.

To send a message:

- Tap the Send Message button. You are presented with this contact's phone numbers and email address to choose from to message. Tap one, and type your message. When you're done, tap Send.

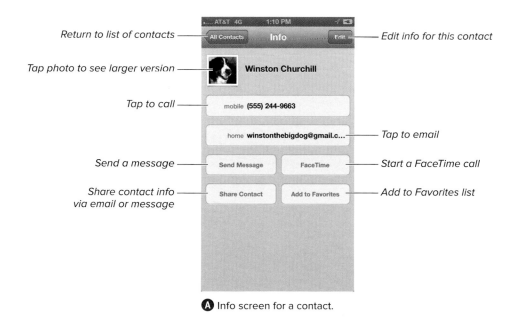

Return to list of contacts
Tap photo to see larger version
Tap to call
Send a message
Share contact info via email or message

Edit info for this contact
Tap to email
Start a FaceTime call
Add to Favorites list

Ⓐ Info screen for a contact.

To share a contact's info:

- Tap the Share Contact button. Choose either Email or Message to send this contact's info to someone 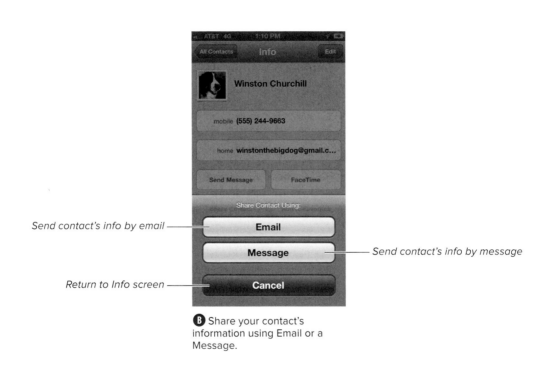 **B**.

To add to your iPhone Favorites:

- Tap Add to Favorites to add this person's phone number to the Favorites listings in the Phone app for easy access.

Send contact's info by email ———— Email

Message ———— Send contact's info by message

Return to Info screen ———— Cancel

B Share your contact's information using Email or a Message.

To search your contacts:

1. Tap in the search field at the top of the All Contacts list.

2. Type any letters in the person's name or any other data field you want to find. As you type, results appear below the search field .

3. Type more letters to narrow your search, or tap one of the results to view a contact.

Type part of the contact info

As you type, search results appear

Tap a search result to view that contact's Info card

C Search your contacts by typing in the search field. Your results appear below as you type.

Adding Mail Accounts

When you add an account to your iPhone, you're tying together your account from a web service like Yahoo!, Google, Facebook, or Twitter to the iPhone apps that can communicate with it. For example, if you connect your iPhone to a Yahoo! account, you'll be able to see all the contacts you've set up in your Yahoo! address book in your iPhone Contacts app. You'll also be able to get and send email from/to Yahoo! If you connect your Facebook account, you'll see all your Facebook contacts in your Contacts app, and you'll see events and birthdays in your Calendar app. Connecting your existing accounts to your iPhone keeps you connected.

To add accounts:

1. Tap Settings > Mail, Contacts, Calendars.

2. Tap Add Account.

3. Tap the appropriate account .

4. Most require an email address and password. Some allow you to add a name for the account or a description.

   Enter the required information and tap Next.

5. You'll see a screen asking you which services from this account you want to use **B**. These options vary depending on the service. Choose On for any services you want available on your iPhone. For example, if you turn on Contacts, addresses and contacts from this service will automatically be added to your Contacts app. If you turn on Mail, a new mailbox will appear in your iPhone's Mail app (learn more about the Mail app in the "Using Mail" section later in this chapter).

6. Tap Save.

A Add Account screen. Choose the appropriate service, or tap Other if it's not listed.

B Choose On for services you want available on your iPhone.

TIP If you have a Yahoo! account, you can import your email, contacts, calendars, reminders, and notes to the matching iPhone apps. Gmail gives you email, calendars, and notes. Other services vary.

To use iCloud for mail and contacts:

1. Tap Settings > Mail, Contacts, Calendars.

2. Tap Add Account and tap iCloud **A**.

3. Enter your Apple ID and Password. (If you haven't created an Apple ID yet, check out Chapter 8, "Getting and Using New Apps" for instructions.) Tap Next.

4. iCloud offers many services **C** to choose from. Tap On for Contacts to integrate your iPhone Contacts app with your contacts on other iCloud-enabled devices. Turn on Mail to use your Apple ID email address to receive mail on your iPhone's Mail app.

Return to the Mail settings

This will display your Apple ID email

Choose which services you want to share with iCloud

C Select your iCloud services.

Setting Up IMAP or POP Accounts

You're not limited to Gmail, Yahoo!, AOL, or Hotmail accounts. You may have an email account through an Internet service provider (ISP) that you want to use. This kind of account is typically either a POP (Post Office Protocol) or an IMAP (Internet Message Access Protocol) account. Ask your ISP which type it is, and request the settings you need to set up your account.

To set up an IMAP or POP mail account:

1. Tap Settings > Mail, Contacts, Calendars.

2. Tap Add Account and tap Other.

3. Tap Add Mail Account.

4. Enter your name, email address, password, and, if you like, a description so you'll know which account this is. Tap Next.

5. Choose either IMAP or POP from the New Account screen Ⓐ.

6. Enter the hostname (provided by your ISP) in the Incoming Mail Server area.

7. Enter your username and password.

8. Enter the hostname in the Outgoing Mail Server area.

9. Enter your username and password again, if required.

10. Tap Next.

TIP If you're not sure about any of these fields, ask your ISP for assistance.

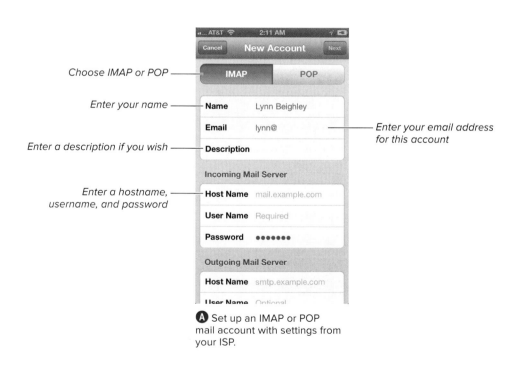

Choose IMAP or POP

Enter your name

Enter your email address for this account

Enter a description if you wish

Enter a hostname, username, and password

Ⓐ Set up an IMAP or POP mail account with settings from your ISP.

Using Mail

 The Mail app **A** lets you send and receive email messages and even view some types of attachments. You can view email you receive in each account you've set up, or all mail in a single inbox.

Setting Up VIPs

You can designate certain email addresses as VIPs and they'll show up in the VIP folder whenever they arrive.

Tap the person's name or address in a From, To, or Cc/Bcc field, and then tap Add to VIP.

Remove them the same way: Tap their name or address and choose Remove from VIP.

You can even assign a special notification so you'll always know when one of your VIP emails comes in under Settings > Notifications > Mail > VIP.

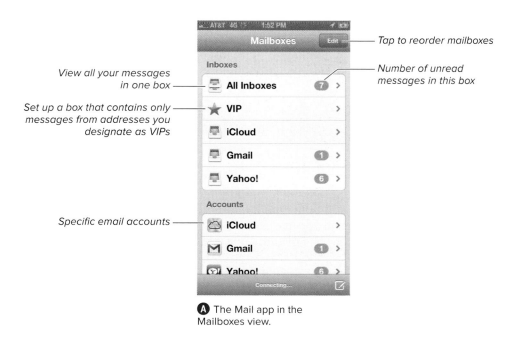

View all your messages in one box

Set up a box that contains only messages from addresses you designate as VIPs

Specific email accounts

Tap to reorder mailboxes

Number of unread messages in this box

A The Mail app in the Mailboxes view.

Getting, Composing, and Sending Mail

Getting, composing, and sending mail on the iPhone is very much how you do so in other mail clients you're already used to.

To get mail:

1. Tap the Mail app in the dock on your Home screen. Mail automatically checks for new messages when you open it. If you have new messages, your iPhone downloads them.

2. Numbers next to listings mean you have new emails in that account. Tap an account to view previews of the messages in that inbox **A**.

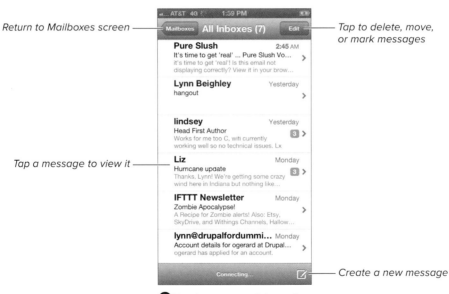

Return to Mailboxes screen

Tap to delete, move, or mark messages

Tap a message to view it

Create a new message

A Preview screen of the mail messages in an inbox.

3. Tap a preview to read a message **B**.

4. Go back to the inbox by tapping the Inbox button, or tap the up and down arrows in the upper right to scroll through other messages in the same mailbox.

TIP As with most iPhone apps, you can tap and drag to scroll if it's a long message. You can spread your thumb and finger or double-tap to zoom in.

Return to the inbox

Tap to view contact info

Tapping and holding on any blue text will open an options screen

Move it to a folder

Flag this message so you can find it later

Open the next or previous message in the inbox

Delete it

Reply to this message

Write a new email

B View of an email message.

Links and Detected Data

There are a number of types of data that your Mail app can recognize in a mail message. If Mail spots an address, phone number, website address, email address, or various other kinds of info, it underlines it in blue.

Tap and hold the link and a pop-up menu appears ❻, offering you appropriate options depending on the link.

Call this phone number with your iPhone

Send a text message to this number

Add this number to your Contacts app

Copy the number to your clipboard

Return to the message

❻ Tap and hold on blue underlined text in a message to see additional options.

To view and save attachments:

1. Open the mail containing an attachment. There's a small paperclip icon in the preview of a message with an attachment.

2. The attachment appears in the body of the message if it's an image, or at the bottom of the message in a gray rounded rectangle **D**. Tap once to view it. (Not all attachment types are viewable.)

continues on next page

Tap and hold to reveal more options ———

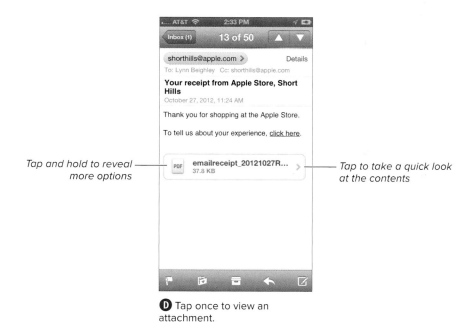

——— Tap to take a quick look at the contents

D Tap once to view an attachment.

3. Tap and hold to see more options **E**.
   These options vary depending on what
   type of attachment it is.

Attachment Types That Open on the iPhone

- Images (JPEG, PNG, GIF, and TIFF)
- Audio (MP3, AAC, WAV, and AIFF)
- Video (M4V, MP4, and MOV)
- PDF, RTF, and text
- Web pages (HTML and HTM files)
  vCard (VCF) files
- Microsoft Office files (Word, Excel, and PowerPoint)
- Apple iWork files (Pages, Numbers, and Keynote)

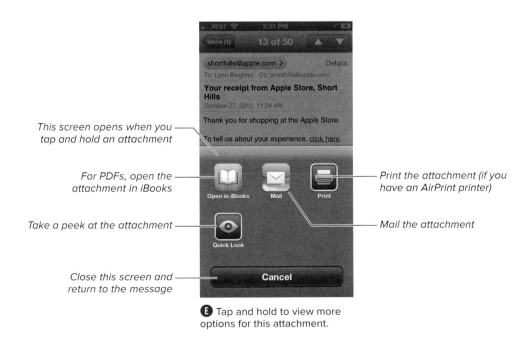

This screen opens when you
tap and hold an attachment

For PDFs, open the
attachment in iBooks

Take a peek at the attachment

Print the attachment (if you
have an AirPrint printer)

Mail the attachment

Close this screen and
return to the message

E Tap and hold to view more
options for this attachment.

To compose and send mail:

1. Tap the new message button on the bottom right of the screen.

   or

   If you're viewing a message **B** and you want to reply or forward, tap the reply arrow and choose either Reply or Forward.

   A New Message (or Message Reply) screen appears **F**.

2. Tap the To field and type the recipient's email address. Or if the recipient is in your Contacts app, tap the blue plus sign to view your contacts. Tap a contact to select it and return to the message view.

   TIP If you accidentally add the wrong recipient's address, just use the delete key to remove it.

continues on next page

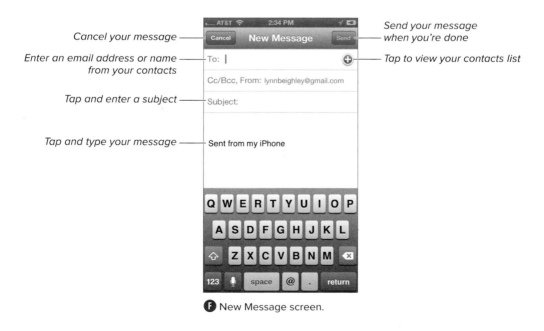

Cancel your message

Send your message when you're done

Enter an email address or name from your contacts

Tap to view your contacts list

Tap and enter a subject

Tap and type your message

F New Message screen.

3. Tap to enter a Cc or Bcc if you wish.

4. If you have multiple mail accounts set up on your iPhone, tap the From field to choose which mail account you want to send this from.

5. Type in a Subject.

6. Tap in the Body section and type your message.

TIP If you want to make some of your text bold, underlined, or italicized, double-tap to select a word, drag the blue dots to select the text you want to change, tap the right arrow in the black menu that pops up, and tap the BIU key.

7. To insert a photo or video from your iPhone's Photos app, tap and hold for a couple seconds, then release. A menu appears. Tap on the right arrow to reveal the Insert Photo or Video option **G**. Tap this.

The Photos app opens. Tap through your images and videos until you locate the one to send. Tap Choose. This returns you to your message with the image or video in the body.

8. Tap Send to send your mail. You can also type Cancel, which offers you the choice to delete the message or save it as a draft to finish later.

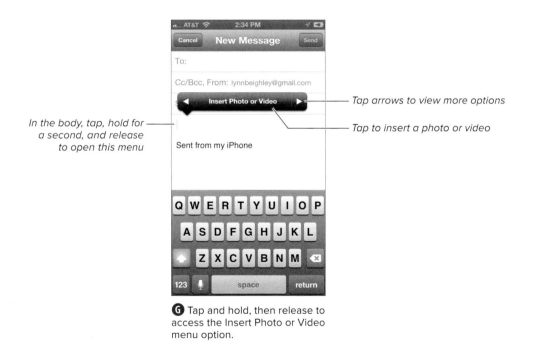

In the body, tap, hold for a second, and release to open this menu

Tap arrows to view more options

Tap to insert a photo or video

G Tap and hold, then release to access the Insert Photo or Video menu option.

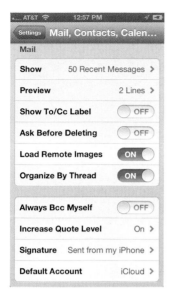

A Mail settings under Settings > Mail, Contacts, Calendars.

Configuring Mail

The Mail app has a number of settings you can change. Tap Settings > Mail, Contacts, Calendars and then change any of the following settings in the Mail section **A**:

- **Show:** This is the number of recent messages each mailbox will display. You can always scroll to the bottom of the list in Mail and view more.

- **Preview:** Controls how many lines of text to display for each message in the preview screen.

- **Show To/Cc Label:** Controls whether or not To and Cc labels appear in the preview list.

- **Ask Before Deleting:** Controls whether or not you must confirm that you want to delete a message.

- **Load Remote Images:** Controls whether images located on a server are loaded by the Mail app when you view a message.

- **Organize By Thread:** Controls whether messages with the same Subject line are grouped in the preview screen.

- **Always Bcc Myself:** Choose this if you want to always get a copy of every message you send. Keep in mind that messages you send are saved in your sent folder, so this may not be useful.

- **Increase Quote Level:** When you reply to a message, this causes the original message to appear indented.

- **Signature:** This line of text is added to the bottom of every mail you send. You can edit it here.

- **Default Account:** If you have multiple mail accounts, this is the one that appears by default in the To field when you compose a message.

Using Messages

 The iPhone includes the Messages app, where you can send both cellular text messages as well as Apple's iMessages. Messages can include audio, video, pictures, and rich text.

TIP When you send a text message, your cellular carrier charges you for it, just as on any other cell phone. Adding images, audio, or video costs even more. iMessages, on the other hand, are free and can be sent to other people you know with newer iPhones and iPads, and even Macs.

To send a message:

1. Open the Messages app on the Home screen **A**. If you've received any text messages or iMessages, you'll see them here.

A Messages screen of the Messages app.

2. Tap the new message button in the top-right corner of the screen. This opens the New Messages screen **B**.

3. You can enter a cell phone number for a non-iPhone user to send a text

   or

   enter the phone number for an iPhone, email address, or Apple ID to send an iMessage.

TIP Or if the recipient is in your Contacts app, tap the blue plus sign to view your contacts. Tap a contact to select it and return to the message view.

4. To add another recipient, tap the To field and start typing.

5. Tap in the text field and type your message, or tap the Microphone and dictate it.

6. Want to send a photo? Tap the photo button and take a photo or choose from photos stored on your iPhone.

7. When you're ready to send your message, tap Send.

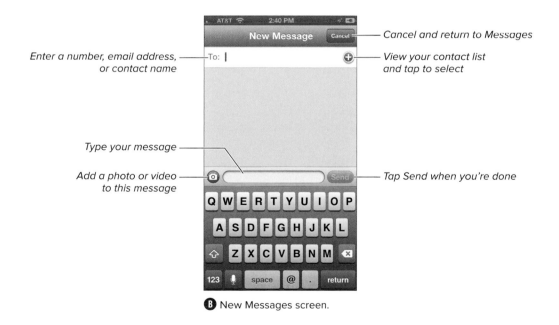

Cancel and return to Messages

Enter a number, email address, or contact name

View your contact list and tap to select

Type your message

Add a photo or video to this message

Tap Send when you're done

B New Messages screen.

Turn Off SMS Messages

It can be difficult to know if you're sending a text message (SMS, and cell companies charge you to send them) or an iMessage (free). By default, your iPhone attempts to send an iMessage. If you never want to be charged for sending text messages because you don't let your iPhone send them, go to Settings > Messages **C** and turn off Send as SMS.

To receive messages:

- When you receive a message, your iPhone will send you a notification. To manage this, go to Settings > Notifications > Messages (See Chapter 6, "Handling Notifications," for more info on these settings).

- To view your messages, tap the Messages app (or the notification alert if you received one). Messages displays all the messages you've received. Unread ones display blue dots **A**.

To reply to a message:

- View the message and type your response in the iMessage or Text Message field at the bottom **B**. Tap Send.

To delete a message or set of messages:

- Tap the Edit button on an individual message, then tap the red minus icon.

- Tap the Edit button from the main Messages screen to delete the entire set of messages back and forth between you and someone else.

TIP You can also swipe your finger to the left or right across the message entry, and tap the Delete button that appears.

C Messages settings under Settings > Messages.

Using FaceTime

 Your iPhone has a front camera, just so you can make and receive FaceTime video calls with other people with compatible iOS devices (and Macs with OS X Mountain Lion).

To set up FaceTime:

1. Tap Settings > FaceTime.

2. Turn FaceTime On **A**.

3. Tap on any of your accounts that you want to be linked with FaceTime. If someone types any of these in their FaceTime app, your iPhone will direct it to you.

TIP You don't need to associate an email address with FaceTime. People who want to use FaceTime with you can use your phone number.

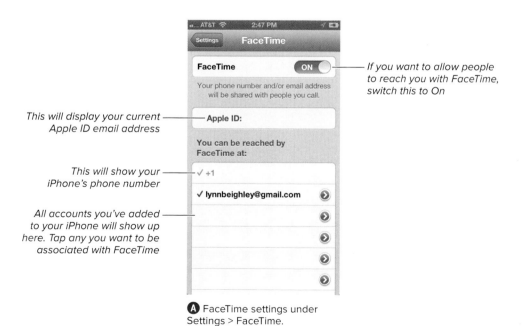

This will display your current Apple ID email address

This will show your iPhone's phone number

All accounts you've added to your iPhone will show up here. Tap any you want to be associated with FaceTime

If you want to allow people to reach you with FaceTime, switch this to On

A FaceTime settings under Settings > FaceTime.

To make a FaceTime call:

1. Open the Contacts app (it's in the Utilities folder). Select a contact and scroll to the bottom of the screen. Tap the FaceTime button.

2. The FaceTime screen appears **B**.

3. When your contact taps the Accept button, he appears **C**. You can begin speaking.

4. Tap on the End button to end your call.

TIP You'll also see yourself in the corner. You can drag your image to any corner of the screen to move it out of the way.

TIP You'll see the FaceTime button to start a FaceTime call in several other places on your iPhone. For example, if you're on a regular phone call you'll see it. And it appears at the top of a message in Messages.

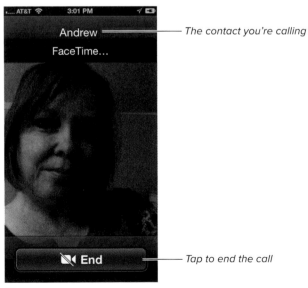

The contact you're calling

Tap to end the call

B FaceTime screen.

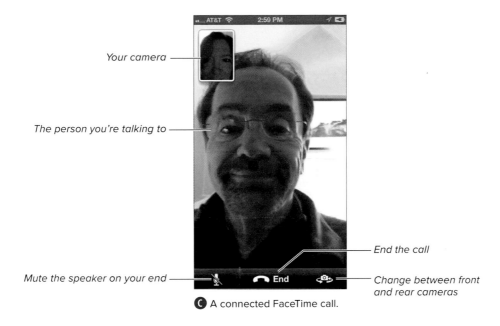

Your camera

The person you're talking to

Mute the speaker on your end

End the call

Change between front
and rear cameras

C A connected FaceTime call.

FaceTime's In-call Options

You can do a number of things during your FaceTime call:

- **Mute the call:** Your caller will see you but not hear you.

- **Switch cameras:** Tap the Camera Swap button to switch between front and rear cameras. Tap again to switch back.

- **Switch apps:** You can open another app, such as Contacts or Notes, during your call. Press the Home button and open the app. Video ends, but audio still works. Tap the green bar at the top to return the video.

Maps, Weather, Stocks, and Clocks

Your iPhone has a smattering of other useful apps that are worth knowing about. In this chapter, you'll take a look at the leftovers.

You'll learn a thing or two about using Maps to find your way, finding out what the day holds with Weather, getting your bearings with Compass, gauging the market with Stocks, and telling time and setting alarms with the Clock.

Using Maps

The Maps app that comes with the iPhone 5 replaces a much-loved Google maps app. It's had some rough times, and the data it contains is still being refined, but you can expect it to improve over time. When you open the Maps app **A**, what you see depends on whether you have Location Services turned on. Maps attempts to find where you are.

TIP Maps works best with Location Services turned on. To do that, go to Settings > Privacy > Location Services and make sure Maps is switched on.

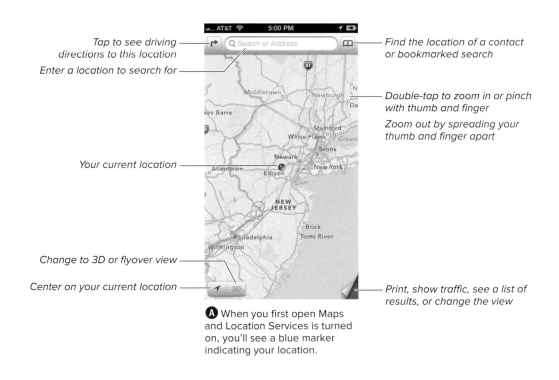

Tap to see driving directions to this location

Enter a location to search for

Your current location

Change to 3D or flyover view

Center on your current location

Find the location of a contact or bookmarked search

Double-tap to zoom in or pinch with thumb and finger

Zoom out by spreading your thumb and finger apart

Print, show traffic, see a list of results, or change the view

A When you first open Maps and Location Services is turned on, you'll see a blue marker indicating your location.

Tap this pin
to see the
location info

B Tap the blue icon in a location banner to view the Location screen.

Gestures to Navigate Maps

- Zoom in by spreading your thumb and finger on the map.

- Zoom out by pinching two fingers.

- Tap and drag to move a map in all directions.

- Place two fingers on a map and rotate to rotate the map. A compass icon appears in the upper right. Tap this icon to return to a northern orientation.

To find places:

1. Tap the search field and type. You can enter:

    • Address

    • Zip code

    • Name of business (Starbucks)

    • Intersection (Main & Elm)

    • Area (SoHo)

    • Landmark (Grand Canyon)

    • Type of business (pizza, bookstore)

2. When you find a location, tap on the arrow to the left of the search box marker to view banner information. Tap on the blue arrow to reveal the Location screen **B**.

To get directions:

1. Find your location by searching for it or entering the address.

2. Tap on the arrow to the left of the search box to open the options for driving directions 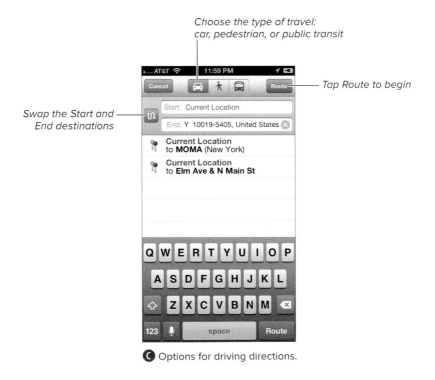.

3. Choose the car, pedestrian, or public transport icon. If you want to change the start and end locations, tap the S-shaped button to the left. Tap Route to see your route options.

4. Tap Start to begin navigating with audible turn-by-turn directions as well as visual directions in Maps.

5. Since your iPhone knows where you are, it detects when you're ready for the next direction and directs you.

To use 3D:

- Zoom in and tap 3D for three-dimensional views of many locations on the map.

TIP Drag two fingers on the screen to aim or adjust the camera view.

To change Maps settings:

- Tap Settings > Maps to see a number of options. These include:

  - Navigation Voice Volume, which lets you choose the volume for your Maps navigation voice.

  - Distances in Miles or Kilometers.

Choose the type of travel: car, pedestrian, or public transit

Tap Route to begin

Swap the Start and End destinations

C Options for driving directions.

Checking the Weather

The Weather app offers you a six-day forecast with the current temperature in Fahrenheit or Celsius and expected highs and low for each day **A**.

TIP Tap the current day's forecast to see an hourly prediction; tap again to return the weekly view.

Swipe right to view the next location's weather

Tap to go to the Yahoo! weather page in Safari

Tap to add new locations

A View the current weather.

To get the weather for where you are:

1. Like so many other apps on your iPhone, the Weather app wants to know where you are. Make sure Settings > Privacy > Location Services has Weather set to On. Tap the Weather app and the default screen is your current location.

2. To get the weather somewhere else, open the Weather app and tap the *i* button on the bottom right **B**.

3. Tap the + sign to add a new location, such as a city name or zip code. Tap on the best result to add it to your weather links.

4. Change from one location to the next by dragging your finger across the screen.

TIP Another way to navigate is to tap to the right or left of the small white dots that appear at the bottom of the screen.

You can always ask Siri what the weather's like. Hold down the Home button and ask her, literally, "What's the weather like?" She'll use your current location and the Weather app to give you the latest.

Tap to add a location

Tap to delete a location

Drag to reorder

Switch to Celsius

B Choose new Weather locations.

Using the Compass

 The Compass app is stashed in the Utilities folder on your Home screen.

To use the Compass:

1. Tap Utilities and then tap Compass to open it **Ⓐ**.

   The Compass shows you the direction it's pointing with a tool that looks like the Boy or Girl Scout compass you recognize.

2. Geographic coordinates (degrees, minutes, and seconds) are displayed at the bottom of the screen. Tap these coordinates to change them to an address.

3. Tap the Location icon on the left. Maps opens with your current location marked. Tap the info button on the bottom right to choose between True North and Magnetic North.

Tap to convert to address

Tap to view current location in Maps

Ⓐ Compass helps you get your bearings.

Checking Stocks

 Use the Stocks app to keep track of your stocks, see the change in value over time, and get news about your stocks. Tap and open the Stocks app from your Home screen **Ⓐ**.

Creating and managing a stock list

Keep an eye on your stocks by adding the ones you want, removing the ones you don't, and ordering them.

- **Add a stock:** Tap the *i* button in the bottom right. Tap the + button on the top left and enter a symbol, company name, fund name, or index. Tap Search.

- **Delete an item:** Tap the *i* button on the bottom right. Tap the red icon to the left of any item you wish to delete. Tap the Delete button.

- **Rearrange the order of items:** Tap the *i* button and drag the handles on the right of an item up or down.

TIP Turn the iPhone to landscape orientation (sideways) and you'll see the current graph enlarged.

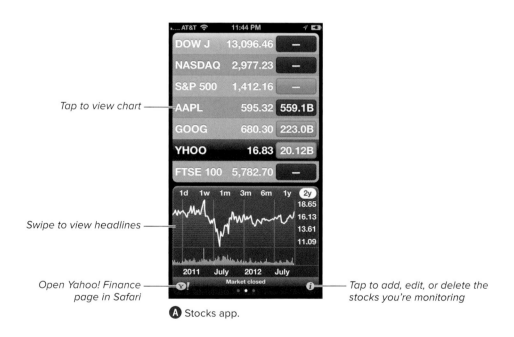

Tap to view chart

Swipe to view headlines

Open Yahoo! Finance page in Safari

Tap to add, edit, or delete the stocks you're monitoring

Ⓐ Stocks app.

A World Clock setting of the Clock app.

Looking at the Clock

The clock on your iPhone is pretty simple and yet useful. You can always see the current time, and you can see times all over the world. Tap the Clock app to open it and tap World Clock **A**.

Using the Clock

Here's how you can customize the clock features:

- Add a new clock to the list by tapping the plus sign in the top-right corner of the screen. Enter the name of a city or country and tap the closest result.

- Remove a clock by tapping the Edit button and then the red delete icon to the left.

- Reorder the clocks by tapping and dragging the handles to the left up or down.

Keeping Time

Your iPhone Clock app lets you keep track of the time you need to get up in the morning, the time it took you to finish running around the block, and the time you're supposed to take your cake out of the oven.

To set an alarm:

1. Tap the Alarm button.

2. Tap the plus icon to add an alarm 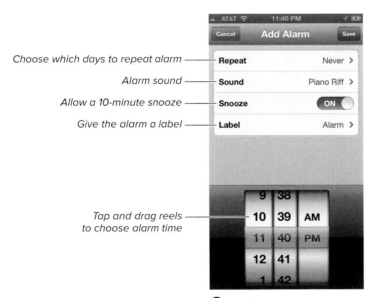.

3. Tap Repeat to choose which days of the week to repeat. Tap all that you wish.

4. Tap Sound to choose the sound you want your alarm to make.

5. Decide whether or not you want to be allowed to hit the snooze on this alarm.

6. Add a label for the alarm if you wish, describing why it's important (it's your birthday or a big important meeting).

7. Tap and drag the wheels around to pick the time you want the alarm to go off.

8. Tap Save.

TIP When you have an alarm set and on, a clock icon appears in the iPhone's status bar.

To set a stopwatch:

- Tap the Stopwatch button, then tap the Start button to begin it. Tap Stop to end it. Tap Reset to reset it.

To set a timer:

- Tap the Timer button. Use the dials to specify how long the timer should be set for. Choose the sound you want to play when time is up. Tap Star to begin the timer.

Choose which days to repeat alarm

Alarm sound

Allow a 10-minute snooze

Give the alarm a label

Tap and drag reels to choose alarm time

A Add Alarm screen.

Extending Your iPhone

You've got all the basics down. You can call, message, chat with Siri, keep track of everything, and set all kinds of tasks. You're up on all the apps that came with your iPhone. But you'd like to do a few more things with it. Maybe use it to play slideshows or movies on your TV with AirPlay. Print directly from it. Use Passbook to manage your tickets, loyalty cards, and coupons. And grab a few more Apple-created apps to make your iPhone even more powerful.

In This Chapter

Using AirPlay

You can use your iPhone with an Apple TV or another AirPlay-enabled device to stream media from your iPhone.

AirPlay lets you stream music, photos, and video to Apple TV and other AirPlay-enabled devices. You can also mirror the contents of your iPhone screen on a TV.

You'll see the AirPlay controls on various apps when an AirPlay-enabled device is available on the same Wi-Fi network that iPhone is connected to.

To stream content to an AirPlay-enabled device:

- Ensure your AirPlay device is on your network. Begin viewing a video Ⓐ or listening to music Ⓑ with your iPhone. Tap the AirPlay button and choose the device Ⓒ.

Ⓐ Viewing a video with the Videos app. If an AirPlay device is on the network, the AirPlay button appears. Tap it to stream the video.

Ⓑ The Music app displays the AirPlay button to allow you to stream music.

C After you tap the AirPlay button, choose the device where you want to stream the media. Tap the button again and choose iPhone to turn off the streaming.

D Press the Home button twice quickly, and then swipe the dock to the right two times to get the AirPlay controls.

To access the AirPlay and volume controls while using any app:

- While using an app during streaming to AirPlay, click the Home button twice quickly and swipe to the left end of the multitasking bar (two swipes) **D**.

To switch off AirPlay streaming:

- Tap the AirPlay button on the app you're streaming and choose iPhone **C**.

To mirror the iPhone screen on a TV:

- Click the Home button twice quickly and swipe to the left end of the multi-tasking bar. Tap the AirPlay button.

You'll see a blue bar at the top of the screen. Everything on your iPhone screen shows up on the TV.

Printing

Yes, you can print from your iPhone. You can print emails, notes, photos, web pages, and many other things. There are two ways to make it work. One is by using AirPrint, a technology that is shipped with some printers.

You must have an AirPrint-compatible printer. HP has been the leading supporter of AirPrint. Look for *AirPrint* on the printer's box.

To use an AirPrint-compatible printer:

1. Hook your printer up to the same Wi-Fi network your iPhone is on.

2. Make sure the printer's AirPrint feature is turned on. Check the manual that came with the printer to do this.

3. Open an app on your iPhone that supports printing. For example, view a web page. Tap the sharing button and tap the Print button .

To see the status of a print job:

- Click the Home button twice quickly. Tap Print Center in the multitasking bar. The red badge indicates how many documents are ready to print.

TIP You can cancel a print job by accessing Print Center, selecting the print job, and tapping Cancel Printing.

TIP The second way to print isn't supported by Apple. It's a third-party software package for your Mac. Visit http://ecamm.com/ and check out Printopia for details on using and purchasing this product.

A Lots of iPhone apps have Print buttons. If you have an AirPrint-capable printer, you're in luck.

Apps That You Can Print From

- **Mail:** Email messages and any attachments that can be opened with Quick Look

- **Safari:** Web pages, PDFs, and anything that can be viewed in Quick Look

- **iBooks:** PDFs

- **Maps:** The map currently displayed on the screen

- **Notes:** The note you have open

- **Photos:** Saved photos

- **Camera:** Photos in your camera roll

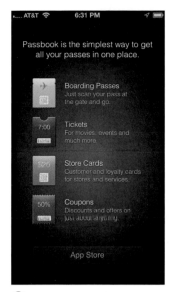

Passbook App

Passbook lets you organize all of your passes, tickets, coupons, and loyalty cards in a single place. Tap a pass to view it.

To get started with Passbook:

- Open the Passbook app **A**. You'll see a promotional screen and a single button, App Store. Tap this button to see the current merchant apps that have support for Passbook. Install any you have an interest in.

To add a pass to Passbook:

- You need to be signed into your iCloud account to add passes to Passbook.

- Adding things to Passbook will vary depending on the vendor. Sometimes you can tap Add to Passbook on their settings screen. You may be able to add a pass from a Passbook-enabled app.

Every vendor will vary in how you set them up, but here's an example that shows how to add your Starbucks card to Passbook. (This assumes you have a Starbucks card.)

To add a Starbucks card to Passbook:

1. Begin by downloading the Starbucks app on your iPhone. Tap Passbook > App Store to open the Apps for Passbook page. Choose Starbucks from the list **B**. Tap Free, and enter your password to install.

2. Open the Starbucks app and log in. Or, create an account and register your card.

continues on next page

A The Passbook app. When you first open it, you have no passes stored. Tap the App Store to see some supported iPhone apps.

B This is a list of App Store apps that integrate with Passbook. They're all free and can be installed from this screen. Tap the Free button, and then the Install button.

3. Tap Card to view your card **C**.

4. Tap Manage. This opens an options screen **D**. Tap Add Card to Passbook.

5. Your Starbucks card will now appear when you open Passbook **E**. You can also see your balance on this screen. Next time you go to Starbucks, open it and scan your card when buying your favorite beverage.

To use a pass:

- Tap Passbook to open it. Select the correct pass and scan it on the merchant's scanner.

C Starbucks is a good example of a card that integrates with Passbook. Go to your card in the Starbucks app to tie it to the Passbook app.

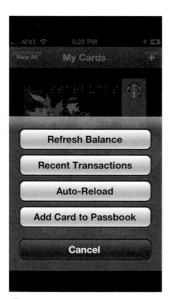

D After you tap Manage, you can choose Add Card to Passbook.

E After you've added your Starbucks card to Passbook, when you open the Passbook app it appears. Quick and easy!

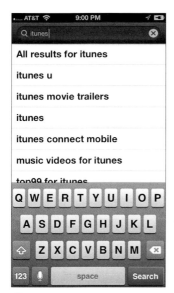

iTunes U App

What's not to like about free stuff? The iTunes U app is full of free education. From leading universities, you can watch, listen to, and learn from lots of courses created by talented, experienced professors. And yes, it's all for free.

To get the iTunes U app:

1. Open the App Store from your Home screen. Tap the Search button on the bottom menu.

2. Type **iTunes U** in the top search box **A**. Tap on the iTunes U listing to open the app screen.

3. Tap the Free button and then the Install button **B**. The app is installed on your iPhone.

A Search for the iTunes U app in the App Store.

B When you've located the iTunes U app in the Search list, tap it to view the listing for it. Tap the Free button.

To use the iTunes U app:

1. After it finishes installing, tap the iTunes U icon on your Home screen.

2. When you first open it, you'll see an empty bookshelf **C**. This is because you don't have any courses downloaded yet. Tap the white sign in the center of the screen to find courses.

3. The iTunes U store opens **D**. Don't worry, these are all free. Drag around, right and left, up and down, to see courses on the Featured screen. Or tap Top Charts, Browse, or Search to find courses of interest to you.

C iTunes U starts with an empty library. Tap the sign in the center to browse courses.

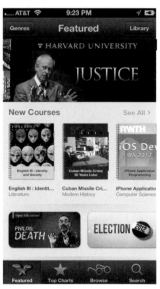

D The iTunes U store. It's organized like the iTunes store because it's a subsite of the iTunes store.

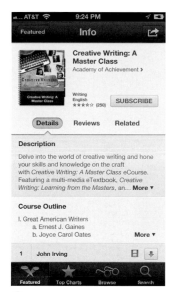

4. Tap a course to see more info about it **E**. If you like it, tap Subscribe. It's then installed in your iTunes U app. Tap the course and begin learning.

To take an iTunes U course:

- After you've installed an iTunes U course, open it in the iTunes U app **F**.

E Tap on any course in the iTunes U store to view more information about it. If you like it, tap Subscribe. It will now show up in your iTunes Library.

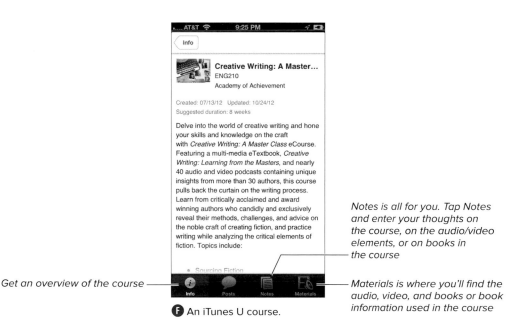

Get an overview of the course ⎯⎯⎯⎯

Notes is all for you. Tap Notes and enter your thoughts on the course, on the audio/video elements, or on books in the course

Materials is where you'll find the audio, video, and books or book information used in the course

F An iTunes U course.

Podcasts App

Just like iTunes U, the Podcasts app is full of free stuff. It's got tons of podcasts containing great ideas, news, and stories.

To get the Podcasts app:

1. Open the App Store from your Home screen. Tap the Search button on the bottom menu.

2. Type **Podcasts** in the top search box. Tap on the Podcasts listing to open the app screen **Ⓐ**.

3. Tap the Free button and then the Install button. Wait while the app is installed on your iPhone.

To use the Podcasts app:

1. After it finishes installing, tap the Podcasts icon on your Home screen.

2. When you first open it, you'll see an empty Podcasts screen **Ⓑ**. Choose between free episodes by tapping on the link in the middle of the screen, or subscribe to existing podcast stations by tapping on Top Stations **Ⓒ**.

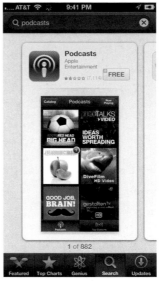

Ⓐ The Podcasts app listing in the App Store. Tap Free and then Install to install it.

Ⓑ Podcasts starts with no saved stations or podcasts. Tap the sign in the center to browse.

3. Drag right and left on the dial at the top of the Tops Stations screen. Drag up and down to see listings for each category.

4. Tap the *i* icon next to a station to see more info about it . If you like it, tap Subscribe. It's then installed in your Podcasts app. Tap Done. Tap the podcast and begin listening.

C Top Stations. Drag the dial near the top of the screen right and left to "tune" the stations—that is, to see different categories of stations. Scroll up and down to see stations in each category.

D More information about a station. If you like what you see, tap Subscribe.

Find My Friends App

 With Location Services on, your iPhone knows where it is. And because it's with you, it knows where you are. If this doesn't make you uncomfortable, and you know your friends feel the same way, you can get the Find My Friends app and locate them whenever you wish.

To get the Find My Friends app:

1. Open the App Store from your Home screen. Tap the Search button on the bottom menu.

2. Type **Find My Friends** in the top search box **Ⓐ**. Tap on the Find My Friends listing to open the app screen.

3. Tap the Free button and then the Install button **Ⓑ**. The app is installed on your iPhone.

Ⓐ Search for Find My Friends in the Search screen of the App Store.

Ⓑ Tap the Free button, then the Install button to install it.

C The Friends screen of the Find My Friends app. From here, you can view where your friends are on the map, and invite more friends by tapping the + sign.

To use the Find My Friends app:

1. The key here is to invite your friends and get them to agree. Open the app and tap the Friends button **C**.

2. Tap the + sign in the upper right and use your contacts or type in emails to send invites to your friends to let you know where they are. They have to accept for this to work.

3. Tap the Friends screen to see the locations of any of your friends who have accepted. Tap on a marker to see who it is.

Find My iPhone App

You were strongly encouraged to use the Find My iPhone features back in Chapter 5, "Managing Your Settings." In that chapter, you learned how to go to iCloud.com to find your iPhone if it's missing.

There's an app for that. If you have a friend with an iPhone, or you have an iPad or Mac, you might want to have this app, which lets you track your missing iPhone (or other Apple device) rather than needing a computer to find it.

To get the Find My iPhone app:

1. Open the App Store from your Home screen. Tap the Search button on the bottom menu.

2. Type **Find My iPhone** in the top search box. Tap on the Find My iPhone listing to open the app screen.

3. Tap the Free button and then the Install button. The app is installed on your iPhone.

To use the Find My iPhone app:

1. Open the Find My iPhone app and enter your iCloud Apple ID and password.

2. You'll see a list of your Apple devices with Location Services switched on, and the Find My service turned on **A**.

A A list of your Apple devices with the Find My service turned on.

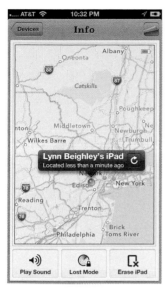

B The map displays the location of your device. You can zoom in and use the options below the map to play a sound, lock your device, or erase it.

3. Tap on the device you want to find. A map opens with your device marked. Choose from a set of options **B**. These are the options your lost device will display:

   Play Sound: Your device will play a sound for 2 minutes so you can find it.

   Lost Mode: Putting your device into lost mode will lock it with a passcode. Lost mode also sends your iPhone a message displaying a contact number. Your device tracks and reports its location to the Find My service.

   Erase: This will erase all information and media on your device. It restores it to original factory settings.

Index